CONCEPTS AND INQUIRY:

The Educational Research
Social Science

Learner-Verified Edition II

COMMUNITIES AT HOME AND ABROAD

Alaska and the Eskimos

Prepared by the Social Science Staff
of the Educational Research Council of America

ALLYN AND BACON, INC.

BOSTON · ROCKLEIGH, N. J. · ATLANTA · DALLAS · BELMONT, CALIF.

This book was prepared by the following members of the Social Science Staff of the Educational Research Council of America:

Ethel K. Howard, Helen Lin, Olga Meyer

Marie M. Richards, *Coordinator K-6*
Agnes M. Michnay, *Managing Editor*

Mary Catherine McCarthy, *Editor-in-Chief*
Raymond English, *Director*

The Educational Research Council of America acknowledges the contributions of the Kettering Family Fund, the Lilly Endowment, Inc., the Martha Holden Jennings Foundation, and the Scaife Family Charitable Trusts, which have made possible the Social Science Program of the Educational Research Council of America.

Cover by BARRY ZAID, PUSH PIN STUDIOS, INC.

Printed in the United States of America

Library of Congress Catalog Card Number 73-90251

5 6 7 8 9 85 84 83 82 81 80 79

Contents

Maps and Globes

Acknowledgments

Photographs: AB ORREFORS GLASBRUK, p. 169 top right. ANCHORAGE HISTORICAL AND FINE ARTS MUSEUM, p. 79 right. AYELSKA PIPELINE SERVICE COMPANY, p. 147. BLACK STAR, p. 169 top middle, Joe Covello; p. 7 left, Tor Eigeland; p.161 bottom left, Thomas Hopker; pp. 154 middle right, 162 left, 167 top right, David Moore; pp. 28, 143, Charles O'Rear; pp. 73, 94 bottom, 96, Joe Rychetnik; pp. 114 top, 115, Arthur W. Woleben. DEPARTMENT OF ECONOMIC DEVELOPMENT, ALASKA, pp. 67 left, 119 right, 149 left. DESIGN PHOTOGRAPHERS INTERNATIONAL, p. 154 right, Morton Beebe; p. 169 bottom left, Phoebe Dunn; pp. 48, 94 middle, Floyd Norgaard; pp. 58 top left, 69 top, 116, Ward W. Wells; pp. 58 middle, 58 bottom right, 114 bottom, 136, 137, 167 top left. DE WYS, pp. 12 bottom left, 77, Luthy. HARRISON FORMAN, pp. 30 left, 40. OWEN FRANKEN, p. 164 top. FRANKLIN PHOTO AGENCY, p. 149 right. FREELANCE PHOTOGRAPHERS GUILD, p. 99 left, H. Johnson. AYLETTE JENNESSE, pp. 113, 134 bottom, 135 bottom. B. J. LAUR, p. 167 bottom left. STEVE MCCUTCHEON, pp. 7 right, 35 top right, 43 right, 53 top left, 53 top right, 58 middle left, 58 bottom left, 58 top middle, 68, 69 bottom, 84, 85, 86 left, 86–87, 90–91, 95, 99 right, 118, 142 left, 142 bottom, 164 bottom, 170 bottom left. MONKMEYER PRESS PHOTO SERVICE, pp. 60–61, 168 top left, Douglas Baglin; p. 30 middle right, Toge Fujihira; pp. 30 top right, 31 top left, 33 left, 35 bottom right, 45, 47, 65 left, 92, 94 top, 100, 101, 102–103, 106, 107, 110–111 bottom, 122, 160 bottom left, 163 right, 168 bottom right, Pro Pix. MULTIMEDIA PHOTOGRAPHY, pp. 142 left, 144, 167 center left, Marvin E. Newman. NAVY DEPARTMENT IN THE NATIONAL ARCHIVES, p. 124 top. NORTHWEST ORIENT AIRLINES, p. 130. RANDALL E. PHILLIPS, pp. 41, 53 bottom, 126. MARJORIE PICKENS, pp. 12 top left, 12 bottom right. RAPHO GUILLUMETTE PICTURES, p. 168 top right, Abbott-Henderson; p. 160 top right, Sabine Weiss. ALLAN ROBERTS, p. 81. G. R. ROBERTS, pp. 43 left, 160 top left, 160 bottom right, 161 top right, 164 middle. SHOSTAL, INC., pp. 78–79, 138 left. DEL STANTON, pp. 65 right, 70–71, 88, 112. STOCK, BOSTON/ELLIS HERWIG, pp. 109, 132 left, 141, 142 top right, 170 top left. TASS from SOVFOTO, pp. 146, 170 (bottom) left top. THREE LIONS, INC., pp. 76, 162 middle, Harrington. UNITED STATES COAST GUARD IN THE NATIONAL ARCHIVES, p. 66 left. UNITED STATES SIGNAL CORPS IN THE NATIONAL ARCHIVES, p. 80.

All photos not otherwise credited are the work of the Allyn and Bacon staff photographers.

Illustrations: EDUCATIONAL RESEARCH COUNCIL OF AMERICA, pp. 89, 97, 116, 117. EROS KEITH, pp. 50, 51, 52, 54, 55, 56–57, 74, 75, 83, 104, 116 top right. TRUE KELLEY, pp. 14, 17, 72. JOHN KUZICH, pp. 8–9, 152–153. MARIE MICHAL, p. 11. LEIGH TAYLOR, pp. 62, 63, 167 center right. KYUZO TSUGAMI, pp. 13, 46.

Map design and compilation by Allyn and Bacon.

A NOTE TO BOYS AND GIRLS

You know some things about the Earth.
You know how some people live on the Earth.
You know that most people live in communities.
You have learned to use social science questions
to find out about communities.   This book
will help you to find out more things
for yourself.

Think about the problems and the questions
as you read.   They are marked ▶, ●, or ★.

This is what the marks mean:

▶   easy to solve,

●   harder to solve — more thinking is needed,

★   something extra — maybe for homework.

Part One

THE ESKIMOS OF NORTHERN ALASKA

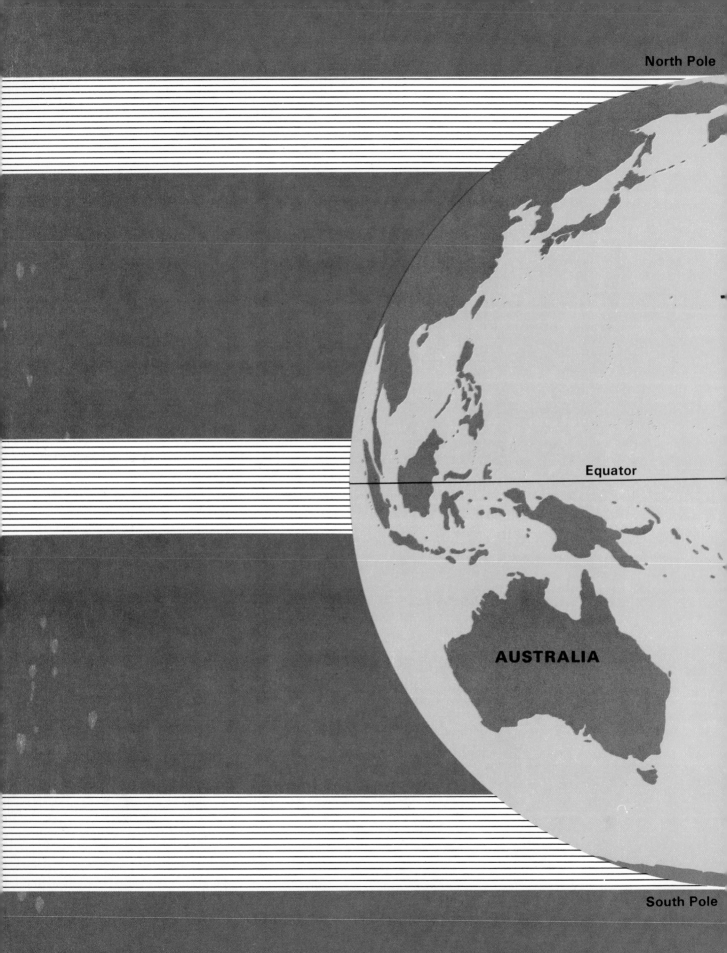

North Pole

Equator

AUSTRALIA

South Pole

CHAPTER 1

More About the Earth and Sun

WHY IS IT ALWAYS HOT
AT MOST PLACES NEAR THE EQUATOR?

Australia is near the Equator. The climate of Australia is warm and dry. The desert Aborigines live in the middle of Australia. The climate of the desert is hot and dry.

Think of the way the sun shines at the Equator. At the Equator, the sun is *high in the sky* most of the day. It *shines straight down.*

▶ What happens to land and water where the sun shines straight down?

▶ Why is it always hot at most places near the Equator?

▶ Is the climate of your community nearly always hot? Is your community near the Equator?

WHY IS IT ALWAYS COLD AT THE POLES?

We are going to learn about Alaska. Alaska is one of the United States. Alaska is far away from Australia. It is closer to the North Pole than to the Equator.

Think of what you have learned about the way the sun shines at the Poles. At the Poles the sun *never* gets high in the sky.

▶ What happens to land and water
where the sun stays low in the sky?

▶ What kind of climate do you think
Alaska has?

The sun in this picture will not get any higher in the sky.
Do you think it was taken in Alaska or Australia?

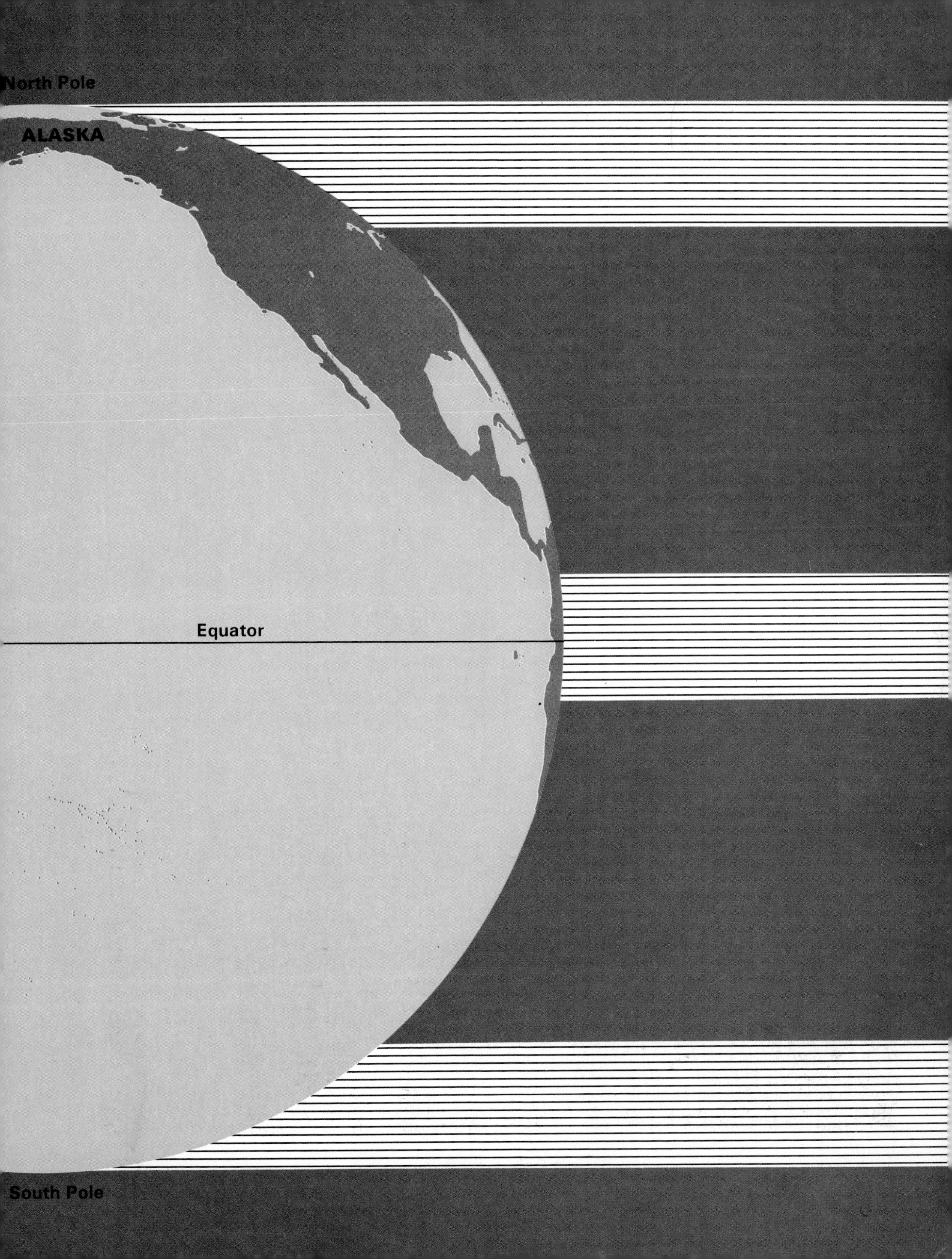

North Pole

ALASKA

Equator

South Pole

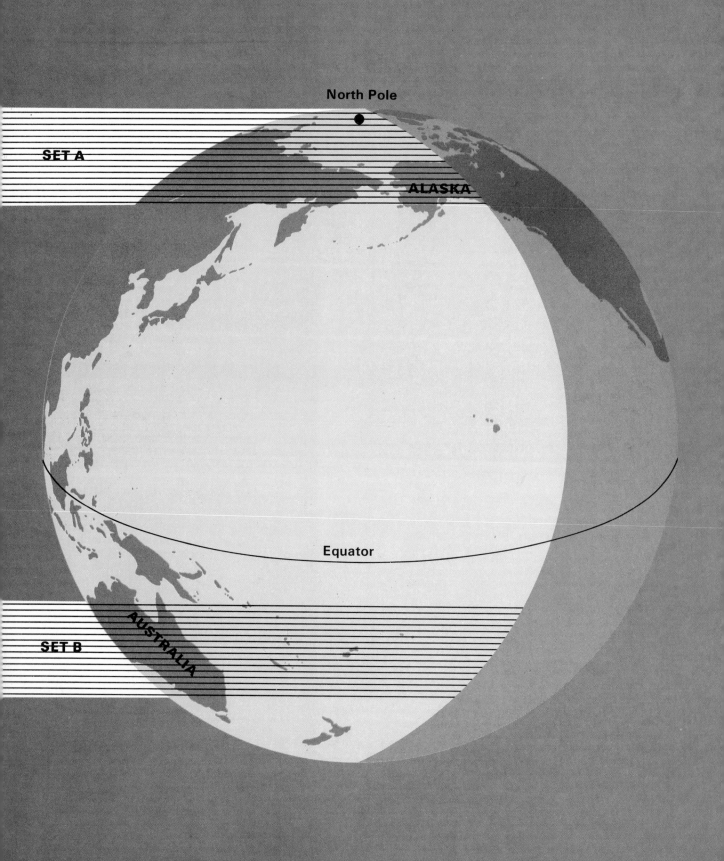

North Pole

SET A

ALASKA

Equator

AUSTRALIA

SET B

Find Australia and Alaska on the globe.

▶ Is Australia near the Equator?

▶ Is Alaska near the Equator?

● Is Australia or Alaska nearer one of the Poles?

● Which place would be colder —
Alaska or Australia? Why?

Which picture shows a place near the Equator?
Which picture shows a place far from the Equator?

Do you remember the rule about the sun's rays?
When the sun *shines straight down* it makes *land
and water warm*. When the sun is *low in the sky,*
its rays *cannot give much warmth.*

Look at the picture of the Earth.

▶ Which set of rays is shining on Alaska?

▶ Which set of rays is shining on Australia?

● Why is Australia warmer than Alaska?

NIGHT AND DAY

Let us find out more about the sun and the Earth.
We know the planet Earth goes round and round the sun.
It takes *one year* to go all the way around.
But the Earth spins while it goes.
It spins like a top.
It spins around once every 24 hours.

● Do you know why we have days and nights?

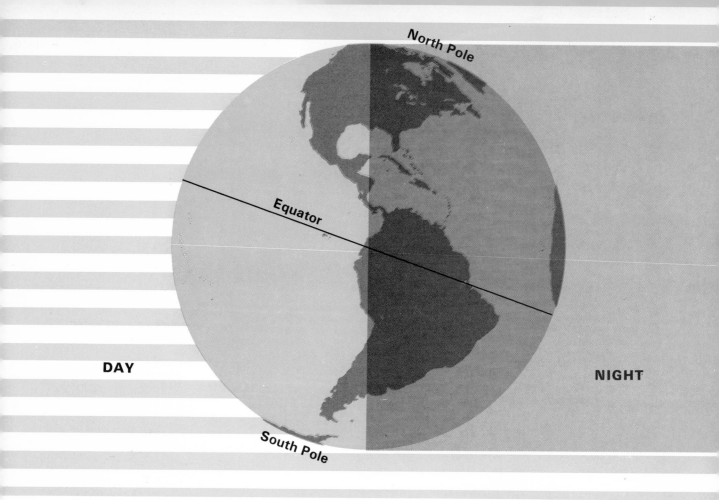

The sun's rays keep coming to the Earth.
But they can shine on only half the Earth at a time.
So the Earth's spin gives us days and nights.
Day comes after night. Night comes after day.
Everywhere in the world there are days and nights.

• Look at the globe. Hold it so that light
  shines on one side. That is how the sun
  shines on the planet Earth.
  Look at the half of the globe that is light.
  That half has day.
  What will the other half have — night or day?

10

• Spin the globe to show when it is day
in North America.

Will it be night or day on the continent of Asia?

• Spin the globe to show when it is day
in Australia.

Will it be day or night in South America? Why?

Summer

Spring

Fall

Winter

LONG DAYS AND SHORT NIGHTS —
LONG NIGHTS AND SHORT DAYS

▶ Does each day of the year have
as much daylight as every other day?

▶ Are winter days as long as summer days?

▶ Are summer nights as long as winter nights?

Think about the seasons. Then try these questions again.

THE SEASONS

Hours of daylight and darkness change with the seasons.

▶ What are the names of the seasons
in most of the United States?

▶ Which season is cold? Which season is hot?

▶ Which seasons are in between the hot and cold?

▶ Which season has long nights and short days?

▶ Which season has long days and short nights?

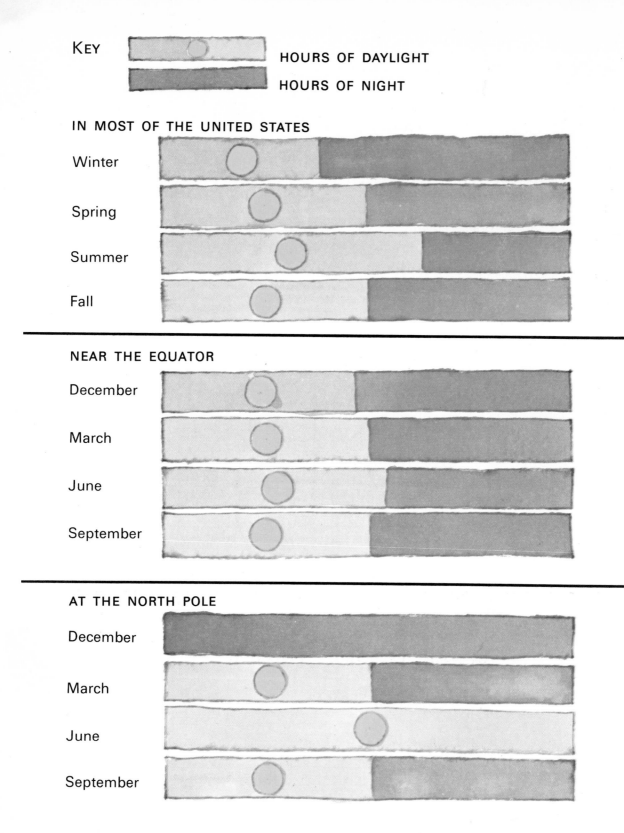

Charts of Daylight and Night in Different Parts of the World

DAYS AND NIGHTS AND SEASONS
IN DIFFERENT PARTS OF THE WORLD

In most of the United States, days are long in summer. They are short in winter.

In some parts of the world, days stay the same all year. Near the Equator, days and nights are almost equal all year long. The sun shines straight down for almost 12 hours in every 24 hours.

But at the North Pole, days and nights are very different in summer and winter.

In summer the sun stays in the sky for months! There is no real night for months at the North Pole.

▶   Guess what happens at the North Pole in winter.

DAYS AND NIGHTS IN ALASKA

Look at the globe to see how near Alaska is to the North Pole.

▶ Which chart of days and nights would be true for Alaska? The one

for most of the United States,

for near the Equator, or

for the North Pole?

In winter Alaska is very cold. The sun is low in the sky for months. In summer Alaska is warmer. The sun is higher in the sky than in winter. But even in summer, Alaska does not get hot.

In northern Alaska in winter, the sun does not shine for months. Winter is like a long, long night.

In northern Alaska in summer, the sun stays in the sky for months. It can be seen even in the middle of the night. Summer in northern Alaska is the season of the "midnight sun."

▶ The sun near the Poles does not make land and water very warm. Tell why.

▶ Which of the pictures above shows the noon summer sun in Alaska?

★ Draw a picture of the winter sun in northern Alaska. That should be easy!

How long is the longest day?
How long is the longest night?
If you will tell me where you live,
I'll try to answer right.

CHAPTER 2
Alaska — Our Biggest State

DIXIE, THE DOG FROM BARROW

Dixie is a husky.   She came from the land
of the Eskimo.   She came from Barrow, Alaska.
Dixie has a thick coat of hair.   She has
pointed ears, dark brown eyes, and big paws.
The big paws help her walk on the snow.

Dixie came to Ohio when she was three years old.
She came to live with her owner, Randy.
She likes Randy very much.   Randy is kind to her.
Randy feeds her every day.

Randy made a little house for Dixie. Randy made a bed of wood beside the house. Dixie sleeps on this bed. It is just like her bed in Barrow.

Dixie wears a collar so that Randy can keep her on a chain. Eskimo dogs in Alaska are kept on chains, too. So this is not new to Dixie.

Dixie obeys her owner. Huskies learn to obey. Then they can work. Dixie will sit or lie down when she is told to. She even lifts her paw to "shake hands."

Can you see the harnesses and collars on these huskies?

Now Dixie lies on a rug instead of on the snow.

Does Dixie like to live in Ohio? Yes. She
is happy to be with Randy. But Ohio is
different from Barrow. In Barrow there is
ice and snow most of the year. The climate is
very cold.

Where is Barrow, Alaska? Let us use a globe
and some maps. They will help us learn
about the place where Dixie used to live.

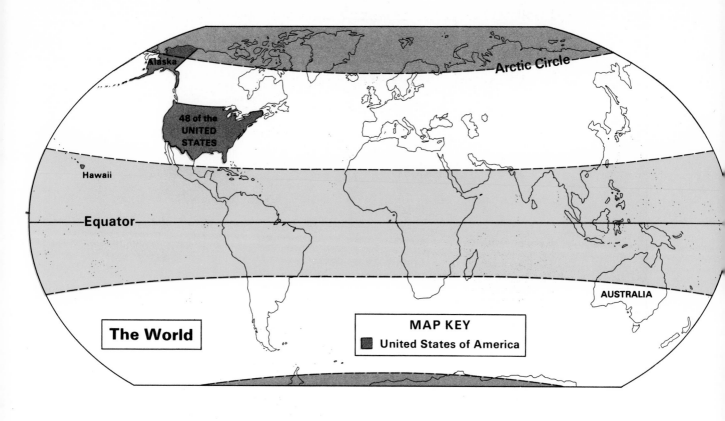

The World

MAP KEY
United States of America

FINDING ALASKA

Look at the map of the world.

▶ Find North America.

▶ Find your country.

● In 1959, Alaska became our 49th state. Find Alaska. What places on the map are the same color as Alaska? Why?

▶ Which part of the United States is farthest north?

Look at the globe in your classroom.

- Find North America. Now find Alaska.
  Move your finger west from Alaska.
  Cross the Bering Strait. Your finger is now
  on the Earth's largest landmass.
  What is its name?

★ What is a *strait?*

- Find the dash line (---) near the North Pole.
  See how it goes through Alaska and Eurasia.
  Trace the line all the way around the North Pole.
  This line is called the **Arctic Circle.**
  All the lands inside the Arctic Circle
  are very cold. They are near the North Pole.
  They are called lands of the Arctic.

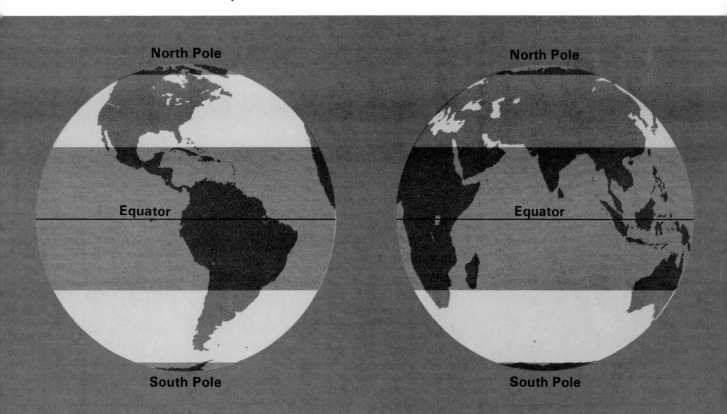

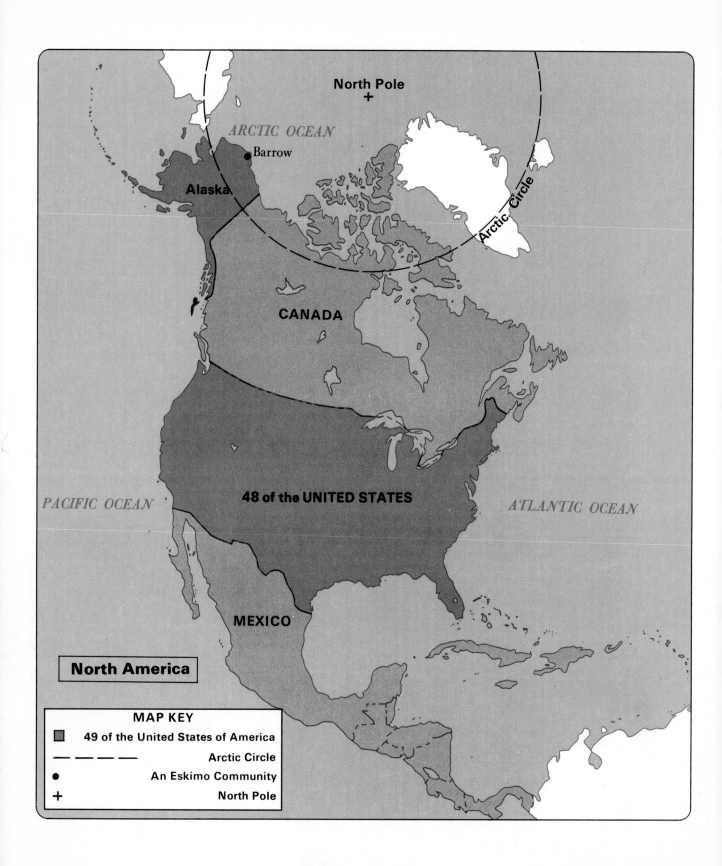

North Pole

ARCTIC OCEAN

Barrow

Alaska

Arctic Circle

CANADA

PACIFIC OCEAN

48 of the UNITED STATES

ATLANTIC OCEAN

MEXICO

North America

MAP KEY

49 of the United States of America

Arctic Circle

An Eskimo Community

North Pole

Look at the map of North America.

▶ Which ocean is east of North America?
Which ocean is west? Which is north?

▶ Name the three big countries in North America.

▶ Find the state of Alaska.

▶ Find the Arctic Circle.
What Arctic lands can you name?

▶ Many Eskimos live in Arctic lands.
The biggest community of Eskimos is
at Barrow, Alaska. Find Barrow.

HOW BIG IS ALASKA?

Alaska is our biggest state. Alaska and its islands
would stretch all the way across the 48 states. It would
stretch from the west coast to the east coast.

Alaska is big. But not many people live there.

▶ Why do so few people live in Alaska?

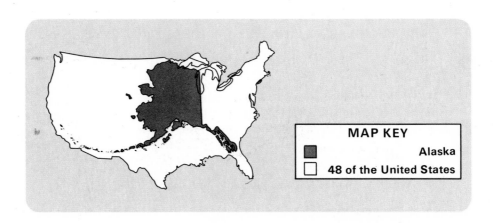

MAP KEY
■ Alaska
□ 48 of the United States

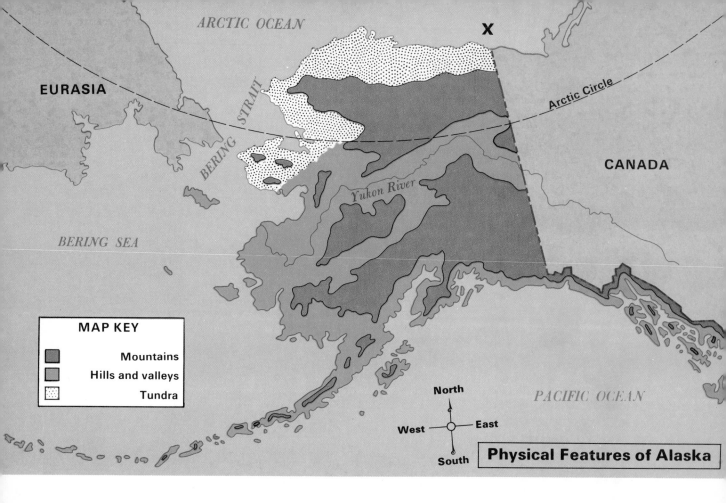

PHYSICAL FEATURES OF ALASKA

Look at the map of Alaska to do this work.

● Alaska is a big peninsula. A **peninsula**
 is a landform that has water on three sides.
 What bodies of water are on three sides of Alaska?
 What country is on the other side of Alaska?

● Find X on the map. Put your finger on it.
 Move your finger along the coast all the way
 around Alaska. You have just traced the **coastline**
 of Alaska. Alaska's coastline is longer than
 that of any other state.

- Use the map key to find mountains. Some mountains are in the southern part of Alaska. The highest mountain in North America is there. The highest mountains are always covered with snow. Find the mountains in northern Alaska. They are also high. Many are covered with snow.

- Between the mountains is a big, big area. It has many hills and valleys. Use the map key to find this area. Big evergreen forests cover the hills. The trees grow part way up the mountains. They cannot grow high in the mountains. The air is too cold. The land is too rocky.

- Along the northern coast is another landform of Alaska. It is low, flat land. This Arctic flat land has a special name. It is called the **tundra.** It is frozen most of the year. No trees grow there. Only small plants can grow on the tundra. Find the tundra on the map.

- Many rivers begin in the mountains of southern Alaska. They flow down through the hills. Find a river that flows into the Bering Sea.

There are valleys between the hills.
Farmers grow fruits, grains, and other food plants
in the valleys.   They raise cows there, too.
The cows give good milk.

Cows grazing in a valley in Alaska

Alaska

Words and Music
by Olga Meyer

A - las - ka, we sa - lute you, The big - gest state of all. Your coast - line is the long - est, Your moun - tains ver - y tall. You have a lot of rich - es. Your peo - ple are so gay. We're proud that you are one of us, Our coun - try U. S. A.

Part of Alaska's long coastline

A stream rushing through a forest

A mountain lake

A glacier — a river of ice

Mountains

A farm in a valley

Waterfall

The coastline of Barrow 31

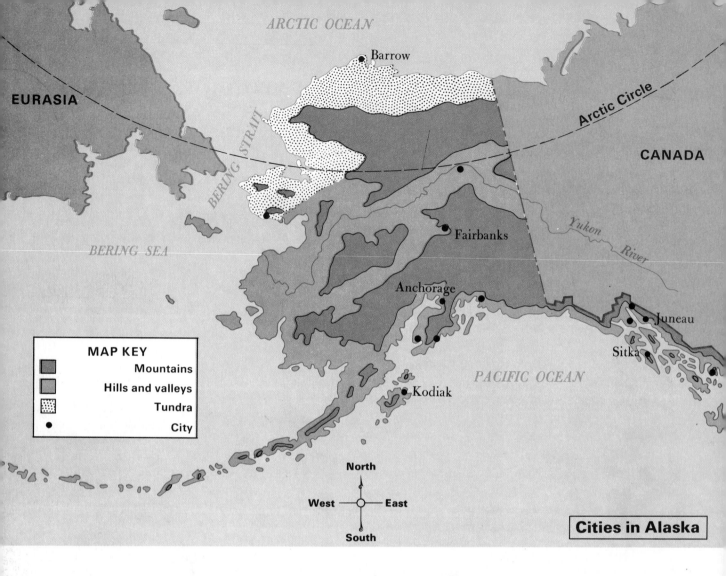

ARCTIC OCEAN

Barrow

EURASIA

Arctic Circle

CANADA

BERING STRAIT

Yukon River

BERING SEA

Fairbanks

Anchorage

Juneau

Sitka

PACIFIC OCEAN

Kodiak

MAP KEY

Mountains

Hills and valleys

Tundra

City

North

West — East

South

Cities in Alaska

CULTURAL FEATURES IN ALASKA

Do you remember that cities are cultural features? How are cities shown on this map?

▶ Find some cities in Alaska.

▶ In what part of Alaska are most of the cities located?

● Are most Alaskan cities north or south of the Arctic Circle? Tell why.

32

Most of the people of Alaska live in the cities.

▶ Find a community on the tundra.

▶ Is most of the tundra north or south of the Arctic Circle?

Most of the Alaskans who live on the tundra are Eskimos.

Barrow –a community on the tundra

Anchorage — Alaska's biggest city

Juneau — the capital city of Alaska

Fairbanks — a city near the center of Alaska

An Eskimo, dressed the way
Eskimos dressed long ago

Eskimo grandmother
and grandfather

An Alaskan family. Are they
Eskimos? How can you tell?
Might they be Indians?

PEOPLE IN ALASKA

Eskimos and Indians live in Alaska. They
have lived there for thousands of years. Many
people in Alaska came from other parts of the United
States.

For thousands of years, Eskimos have lived on
the western and northern coasts of Alaska. We shall
study the Eskimos of northern Alaska. Let us visit
some Eskimos who live north of the Arctic Circle.
We will go to the place where Dixie was born. We
will visit the community of Barrow.

Alaskan Indian children

An Eskimo boy and his huskies

This person came to Alaska to find gold.
What is he doing?

3
North to Barrow

ALASKA, HERE WE COME!

How will you get to Alaska from your home?
You may fly from Seattle, Washington.

▶ How will you get to Seattle
from your community?

From Seattle, you take a plane to Fairbanks.
Flying is the best way to travel in Alaska.
Alaska has few roads. That is because it has
so many mountains. And it is covered
with ice and snow most of the year.
From Fairbanks you will go to Barrow.

▶ Find Barrow on the map.

▶ How will you travel to Barrow?
FIRST CLUE: no roads to Barrow.
SECOND CLUE: no railroad tracks to Barrow.
Can you guess?

NORTH OF THE ARCTIC CIRCLE

To Barrow, to Barrow
    We'll fly in a plane,
It's too far to walk,
    And there isn't a train!

The pilot of your plane is helpful and friendly.
The pilot talks to you after the plane is in the air.
"We are leaving Fairbanks," says the pilot.
"People call Fairbanks the 'Golden Heart' of Alaska.
That is because it is the center of the gold mining area.
Now you can see Alaska's big evergreen forests below."

All at once you feel the plane go down a bit. The pilot says, "Look! Now you are flying over the Arctic Circle."

You look and look but you cannot see a circle. The pilot laughs. You laugh, too, as you remember something about the Arctic Circle.

▶   Why can't you see the Arctic Circle?

▶   Find the Arctic Circle on the globe.
    Tape a piece of yarn on the line. Put the globe on the floor and look down at the North Pole. Inside the yarn circle you will see the "lands of the Arctic."

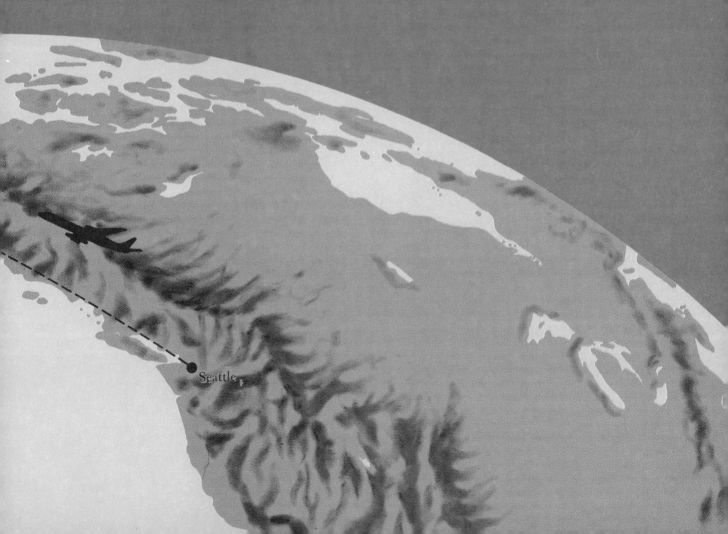

Seattle

Trees grow part of the way up these mountains.
Why don't they grow all the way to the top?

WHAT IS PERMAFROST?

The plane climbs higher in the air.
Alaska's northern mountains are ahead.
"Soon we will be flying over the mountains,"
the pilot says.
The pilot asks, "Do you see the tree on your right?
That is the last tree you will see from here on."

The pilot is not joking. There are no more trees. You have just passed the **tree line.** Of course, there is no line. But you can see where the trees have stopped growing. North of the tree line, it is too cold for trees to grow.

All of northern Alaska is a land of **permafrost.** This means the ground is frozen as hard as a rock most of the year. For a short time in the summer, the frozen ground thaws a little. In some places, the people can dig down only one or two inches. Then they hit frozen earth.

Eskimos chop holes in the frozen ground. They use these holes just as we use freezers. Eskimos put meat in their "freezers." The meat stays good to eat for a long time.

Why don't trees grow on this part of the tundra?

The pilot flies the plane over the mountains.
See how the land slopes down to the Arctic Ocean.
Rivers start in the mountains. They zigzag down
across the land. At last they reach the ocean.

The land between the northern mountains
and the Arctic Ocean is the tundra.

An Eskimo boy on the tundra in summer

The tundra is flat. In winter, you cannot see
where the tundra ends and the ocean begins.
It is all under ice and snow.

▶ Find the tundra, the Arctic Ocean,
and the northern mountains on the globe.

A hot desert   A cold desert

THE CLIMATE ON THE TUNDRA

On the tundra the climate is cold and dry.
There is very little rain. There is no more rain than
on the Australian desert. There is not even much snow.
This land may be called a **cold desert.**

The tundra in summer

There is little rain and snow. But when snow
comes, it stays for months and months.

The snow on the tundra is dry. It is like powder.
Strong winds blow the snow into big drifts.
The drifts make it look as if there is much snow.

▶ Why is the tundra called a cold desert?

44

The weather is so cold that the snow stays
on the ground all winter. It does not melt until summer.

In summer, the frozen ground thaws a little.
The tundra is wet and muddy. Small plants grow
in the wet soil above the permafrost. The
permafrost is just under their roots.

★　What does *permanent* mean? Can you see
　　why we use the word *permafrost?*

The tundra in winter

Winter, about six months.

Spring, about two months.

Summer, about two months.

Autumn, about two months.

THE SEASONS ON THE TUNDRA

When does winter begin? When does it end?
On the tundra it is hard to tell. The change
comes very, very slowly. It comes so slowly that you
hardly know the weather is changing.

In winter, the sun does not rise at all
for about 65 days. When there are no rays
from the sun, land and water become very cold.

Then the long dark months are over. One day
the sun rises just a tiny bit. Each day it rises
a tiny bit higher. But never does the sun
rise high in the sky. Not even in summer.
It rises only about halfway. So even the summers
do not get very warm.

Do you like to go to bed when it is dark?
If so, it would be hard to go to bed in Barrow
during the summer. You can see the sun
both day and night! It does not set for about 75 days.
On those days you can see the sun at midnight!

▶ Why is summer in northern Alaska
  called the season of the midnight sun?

The midnight sun

4

Some Animals of the Arctic

THE CARIBOU

Caribou (KAIR i boo) are a kind of deer.
They live on the Arctic tundra. Their big feet
are just right for walking in snow or mud. Both father
and mother caribou have big bony antlers. Once a year
the caribou shed their antlers. Then they grow new ones.

The caribou spend much of their time eating.
In summer they go north across the tundra.
They eat small plants, grass, and leaves. In winter
they go south. They look for reindeer moss.
Caribou are sometimes called "scratchers."
They use their feet to scratch away ice and snow.
Then they can find reindeer moss.

SEALS

This is a spotted seal. Part of the year, seals live in the Arctic Ocean. They swim as fast as lightning. They swim and dive to catch fish.

The Arctic Ocean is cold. But seals have a thick layer of fat all over their bodies. This fat is called blubber. The blubber keeps them warm in the ice-cold water.

Instead of legs, seals have flippers. They have two flippers in front and two in back. Their back flippers are joined together. They move like the tail of a fish. They help seals to swim.

Seals do not stay in the water all the time. When summer comes, they like to lie on top of the ice. They lie there in the sun. But they must be careful. When they are on the ice, they cannot move very fast. Then it is easy to catch them.

When winter comes, the water begins to freeze. Seals make holes in the ice. These are breathing holes. Seals keep these holes open as long as the water is frozen over. Seals can stay under water about 20 minutes. Then they must come up to breathe.

Some seals are big. Spotted seals are small. One spotted seal weighs about 100 pounds.

OOGRUKS

There is another kind of seal. It is big! It may weigh as much as 800 pounds. Its skin is very tough. It has a beard. It is an oogruk (OO gruk), or bearded seal.

★ Find out how much you weigh. Now you can guess how much bigger seals are!

THE WALRUS

This animal looks something like a seal. It is
a walrus. It lives in the Arctic waters, too. It is
even bigger than the oogruk. It may weigh as much
as 3,000 pounds.

★ Ask your parents how much their car weighs.
Does a walrus weigh more
than your parents' car?

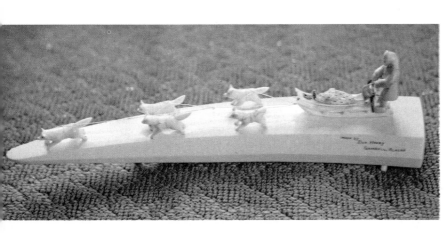

Eskimos carved these things from walrus tusks.

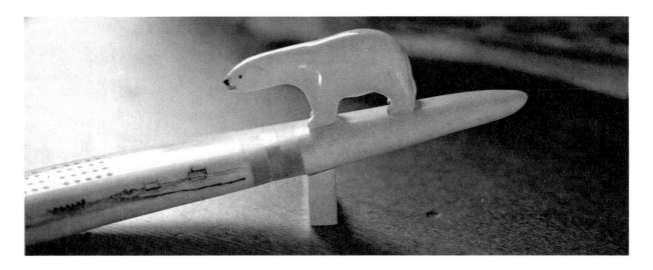

A walrus has two long ivory tusks. It uses the tusks to fight. It uses them to dig for food at the bottom of the ocean. It also uses them to pull itself onto the ice.

A walrus has flippers like a seal. But the walrus's back flippers are not joined together. So when it is on land, the walrus can walk on its back flippers. It walks the way a duck does. How funny it looks!

THE POLAR BEAR

The polar bear is big and strong. It is not afraid
of other animals. Its home is on top of the ice in
the Arctic Ocean.

Cold weather does not bother the polar bear. It
has a thick coat of white fur. The fur is oily.
The oily fur helps to keep the bear dry when it swims.

A polar bear is hard to see on the ice and snow.
Its white fur helps to hide the bear when it hunts for food.
Can you guess what food the polar bear hunts?

Seals and walruses and fish!

THE ARCTIC FOX

The Arctic fox has beautiful white fur. The fox likes to eat rabbits. In fact it eats every little animal it can find.

In summer, it is easy to find lots of food. The fox eats until it is quite full. Does it stop hunting? Oh, no! It kills more little animals. It saves them for winter, when food is hard to find. The fox saves the animals by burying them.

The Arctic fox has another way to get food in winter. It watches for a polar bear catching a seal. Sometimes it helps the bear to find a seal. The fox knows that the bear will not eat all of the seal. There will be enough left over. Then the fox can eat some seal meat, too.

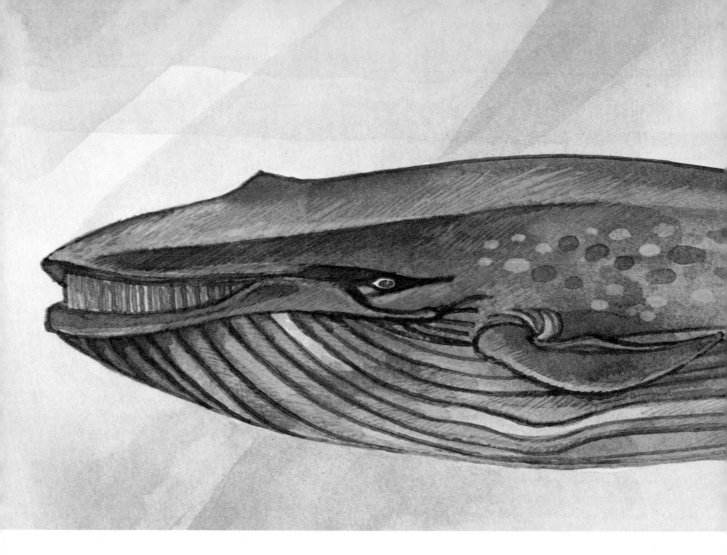

THE WHALE

Did you ever see such a great big mouth?
The whale uses its mouth to get food. It
swims up to a lot of little plants that grow
in the water. Tiny sea animals live among
these plants. The whale opens its big mouth
and it fills up with food.

▶   What two kinds of food does the whale get
     this way?

Do you see something hanging down in the whale's
mouth? It is called baleen. This whale is called a baleen
whale. When its mouth is full of food, the baleen
works like a strainer. The baleen lets the water go out
of the whale's mouth. But it holds the food in.

Whales are the biggest animals alive. Whales
that swim in the Arctic Ocean have a thick layer
of fat, or blubber. The blubber keeps them warm
in the cold water.

CHAPTER 5
The Eskimos —
People of the Tundra

THE ESKIMOS

Long ago there was land connecting Eurasia and Alaska. Some Eurasians must have walked over this land bridge to Alaska. Those people were the first Americans.

On the cold tundra, it was hard to get food. The first Americans soon moved south.

Later, some people stayed on the tundra. They came by boat. They must have been strong and clever. They learned how to live in the Arctic. They were Eskimos.

● The first Americans were the ancestors of some people who live here today. What do we call these people?

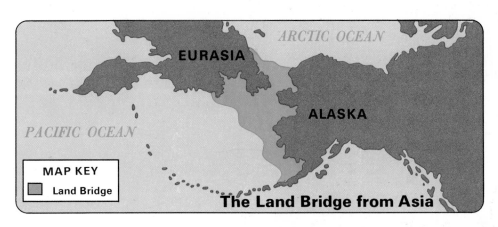

The Land Bridge from Asia

An Eskimo hunter spearing fish
in Alaska

An Aboriginal hunter in Australia

Eskimos have light brown skin. They have dark brown eyes and black hair. Their hands and feet are small. Eskimo hunters and fishers need to be strong. They need to be skillful, too.

● Look at the pictures of Eskimos in this book. The Eskimos are part of a very large group of people. The group is called **Mongoloid.** Look at the eyes, skin, and hair of the Eskimos. What other people do you know with Mongoloid features?

Some Eskimos still live as their great-grandparents did. They hunt and gather food. They move from place to place. They do not build cities. They make their own weapons and tools.

Today Eskimo communities are changing. They have been changing fast. We will learn how an Eskimo community has changed.

Let us think back to times long ago. How did Eskimos live on the tundra then? How did they use the tundra? How did they use the Arctic Ocean for the things they needed? We will find out. Then we will see how Eskimos live on the tundra today. We will see how their way of life has changed.

● Find the Bering Strait on the globe. Trace the route the Eskimos may have taken in their boats.

Inside an igloo

IGLOOS

All Eskimo houses were once called **igloos.**
Eskimos built igloos from whatever they could find.

The Eskimos on the tundra built frames
for their igloos. They made the frames of driftwood
or whale ribs. Driftwood is wood that drifts up
on the beach in summer. They covered the frames
with chunks of sod. Sod is earth held together
by the roots of grass and plants.

A hole was left in the top of each igloo. The hole
let in fresh air and light. In very cold weather,
the hole was covered with sealskin.

A long tunnel led into the igloo. It was so low
that the Eskimos had to crawl in on hands and knees.
The long, low tunnel kept cold winds out of the igloo.

• Why didn't the Eskimos cut down trees
  to make their igloos?

The outside of an igloo

An Eskimo stone lamp was shaped something like a bowl. Oil was poured into the lamp. A wick was placed in the oil and lighted.

Eskimo lamps burned seal oil or whale oil. The lamps made the inside of the igloo warm. Sometimes it was very warm. The Eskimos did not need to wear their fur clothes inside.

They built a long bed along the back of the room. They covered the bed with grass or animal skins. This is where the whole family slept.

Arctic cotton was used as a wick in the lamp.

PARKAS, PANTS, AND MUKLUKS

Men, women, and children wore the same kind of clothing. It was made from the skins of animals. Fur jackets were called parkas. Mukluks were Eskimo boots. Eskimos also wore fur pants and mittens.

During the winter, the people wore two suits. They wore the first suit with the fur on the inside. They wore the second suit with the fur on the outside. Do you see why they would take these clothes off inside a warm igloo?

▶ Where do you get the clothes you wear?

● Where do you think the Eskimos used to get their clothes?

Some Eskimos today still wear clothes like those of long ago. Find the parka, mukluks, and pants.

Some Eskimo women still chew sealskin to make it soft.
What do you think this does to their teeth?

All the Eskimos' clothes were made
by the women. What a job that must have been!
First the animal had to be skinned. The inside
of the skin was scraped. The snow was used
to scrub it. As the skin dried, it became stiff.
To make it soft, the women would chew it
and chew it. Some women had chewed many skins.
Their teeth were worn down.
After the skin was soft, the women used knives
to cut it into pieces. They sewed the pieces together
by hand to make new clothes. They used a needle
made of bone. For thread they used sinew
from the caribou.

The Eskimo women had another hard job.
They had to keep everyone's clothes mended
and dry. When clothes got wet, they had to be dried.
Then the women had to chew them until they
became soft again.

▶ Do you have a parka?

▶ Are some of your winter clothes
like Eskimo clothes? Are they made
of the same things?

These Eskimo women are making mukluks by hand as women did long ago.

HOW DID ESKIMOS
LEARN TO LIVE ON THE TUNDRA?

Let us think of when the Eskimos first came
to live on the tundra.   There was no town of Barrow.
The Eskimos could grow no food.   There were
few things they could use to build houses.
The weather was very cold.   Only animals
with thick fur could live there.

The Eskimos found a way to live on the tundra.
They used the animals living there for food and clothing.
Sometimes they used the animal skins for shelter.
They learned to use their natural environment.

▶   How did the Eskimos use
their natural environment?

Let us find out more about how Eskimos lived long ago.

How do these pictures show that the Eskimos learned to use
their natural environment?

CHAPTER 6

A Year on the Tundra Long Ago

SEASONS ON THE TUNDRA

Let us see how the Eskimos lived on the tundra long ago. We will pretend to go through a whole year with them.

On the tundra the seasons are very different from ours. We will not talk about winter, spring, summer, and fall. Instead, we will talk as the Eskimo talks:
> about daylight months,
> break-up months,
> growing months,
> freeze-up months,
> and dark months.

Remember what we learned about the sun.
North of the Arctic Circle, here is how the sun looks
at noon.

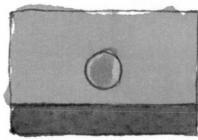

During the *daylight months*
it is just above the skyline.

During the *break-up months*
it is a bit higher.

During the *growing months*
it is halfway up the sky.
It does not set at all.

During the *freeze-up months*
it is lower in the sky.

During the *dark months*
it gets lower and lower, until . . . for a long time
                              it does not rise at all.

Since there were no cameras long ago, this and other pictures show people, places, and things of today. Still the pictures help show how Eskimos lived long ago.

THE DAYLIGHT MONTHS

Our "pretend" year on the tundra begins with the daylight months. These are the months when daylight comes back to the tundra. The long, dark winter is over.

We will read about Akpik and his family. We will learn how they hunted animals for food, clothing, and shelter. We will even learn something about the animals.

WAITING FOR A MEAL

Here we are on the coast long ago. This is where the tundra ends and the ocean begins. Let us stand very still. Look way out on the ice. What is that black spot out there? It is a spotted seal!
It has just come out of its breathing hole in the ice.
The daylight months have come again. The sun is shining low in the sky. The seal goes to lie in the sun. It goes to sleep beside the breathing hole. Seals do not sleep for long. Someone may be out hunting them.

The spotted seal often wakes up to look around. If everything is quiet, it takes another nap. When it is hungry — splash! Down it goes through the breathing hole

to catch some fish. Then up it comes again. It lies beside the breathing hole. It takes another nap.

Soon the seal raises its head to look around again.
Oh! What is that? It sees something move a wee bit.

What is it? An Eskimo hunter? A bear hunting for some food? The seal does not wait to find out. Splash! Down it goes through the breathing hole.

The seal was right. Something is moving nearby. It is a polar bear. The bear is big. But it is white and hard to see. It is lying flat on its tummy. It uses its claws to pull itself slowly and quietly toward the seal. The seal is lucky to have moved when it did! The bear would have had a fine seal for a fine meal.

Do you think the bear will give up and go away? Oh, no! It will not give up so soon. It will stay right beside the breathing hole. The bear knows that soon the seal will have to come up for air. So it will just wait until the seal comes up again.

Now let us look back to the flat, snowy tundra.
See those big humps? They look like hills of snow.
What could they be? Look. An Eskimo is coming out
of one of them. They are igloos!

The Eskimo is called Akpik. He walks up to seven other
little humps. They are also covered with snow.
"Up, up!" he shouts. Suddenly the humps come alive.
Each one was a sleeping husky dog. A husky dog
sleeps all curled up with its tail over its nose.
This way it stays as warm as toast.

As soon as Akpik shouts to the huskies,
they are up and howling. How they love to go on trips!
They roll in the snow. They howl and jump.
"Yip, yip, yip, yip!" Such yipping and yelping
you have never heard! The dogs can hardly wait
until Akpik has put the harness on them.

Soon he is ready. The dogs are harnessed two by two. The lead dog is harnessed to the other dogs. But it is the guide. It must go in front, all by itself. Akpik stands behind the dogs, at the end of the long sled. He shouts and cracks his whip. Away they go!

The dogs dash away. Akpik has to hang on tight or he will fall off. He shouts to the lead dog. The dogs all slow down to a trot. They are so strong! It is easy for them to pull the sled over the ice and snow.

Akpik is going to look at the traps he has set on the tundra. He goes to look at them every day. How excited he is when he finds an animal or a bird in one of them!

Today Akpik is very excited. In one trap he finds an Arctic fox. The fox has beautiful white fur. Akpik's wife Pamiok will be glad to have the fur. She will use it to make trim for their little girl's parka.

Look at the dogs now! They are sniffing the air. Akpik knows this is a good sign. Huskies have very good noses. He cracks his whip. Away they go like the wind! What do you think they smell?

An Eskimo spear maker. The spears are used for birds, seal, and walrus.

BRINGING HOME THE MEAL

Do you remember what the bear was doing?
It was waiting at the breathing hole. The bear was
waiting to grab the seal when it came up for air.

The huskies can smell the bear. Off they go
across the ice. Akpik stands on the sled behind them.
He grabs his spear. Now he can see the bear.

Oh, oh, the bear is running away! It is not afraid
of one animal. But there are eight animals running toward
it. The bear knows it had better run for water. If it
can get to water, it will jump in and swim away. But the
bear will not get away. The huskies are too fast.

Akpik stops the sled. He quickly unhitches the dogs.
Before you know what has happened, the dogs have made
a circle around the polar bear. How angry it is! How
fierce it looks! It stands up on its hind feet. It tries
to hit the huskies with its big front paws. One of the
blows would kill a dog. But the huskies move fast.
The bear cannot hit them. The dogs rush at the bear,
nipping at its legs.

Now Akpik comes running. He kills the bear
with his spear. He puts the bear's body onto the sled.
Akpik hitches up the dogs again. Off they go.

The seal has been waiting at the breathing hole.
It has been waiting till everything was quiet. Now
it is out on the ice again. It will take another nap
in the fading sunlight.

Akpik is on his way back to the igloo. He is happy.
Tonight his family will have a fine meal of bear meat.
The dogs will have a fine meal, too. And before long,
the bearskin will be a warm cover for someone's bed.

Akpik has to spend most of his time hunting for food.
Everyone on the tundra has to do the same.
Many days Akpik comes back without food on his sled.
Today, he has been very lucky.

▶   How many kinds of food
     have you read about in this story?

▶   Why does Akpik kill animals
     instead of growing food?

Akpik and Pamiok have three children.
Tingook is the oldest child.   He is 12 years old.
He helps Akpik every day.   Tingook has a sister,
Nathlook.   She is seven.   She is learning
to help her mother.   Then there is baby Koahk.
He is only a year old.   He rides in the back
of his mother's parka.   Her parka is made to hold a baby.

An Eskimo mother and her baby today.   Pamiok probably carried
Koahk this way, too.

Do you know how Koahk got his name?
Pamiok heard noises one night.   She thought that
the noises were made by the spirit of someone who
had died.   Pamiok wanted to please the spirit.

Long ago, Akpik and his family lived in a sod igloo like this one.

So she gave her baby the name of the dead person.
That is how Koahk got his name. Eskimos
are named after someone who has died.

During most of the year, Akpik and his family
live near the coast. They live in a sod igloo.
The number of people who live in the igloo may change.
Akpik's brother and his brother's family may come
to live in it. Maybe his mother will come to live in it
for a while. Many people may live in the igloo.
But Akpik is the head person of the whole family.

These pictures show Eskimo women doing jobs just as they were done long ago. (left) An Eskimo woman splitting a skin.   (right) Eskimo women covering an umiak.

THE UMIAK — A BIG BOAT

In the daylight months the sun rises higher.
The days are getting brighter and brighter.
That is a sign to Akpik and the other Eskimos. It is time
to get their umiaks ready for hunting and traveling.

An umiak (OO mee ak) is a big boat. It can hold
12 people. The Eskimos use paddles to move it swiftly
through the water. The frame of the umiak is made
of driftwood. It is sometimes covered with big oogruk skins.

The women help to get the umiak ready
for hunting whales.   They sew new skins together.
Then the Eskimos take the old skins off the wooden frame.
They stretch the new skins on it.   This is hard to do.
But afterwards the boat is like new again.

The umiak is a fine boat.   It is not heavy.
It is safe for women and children to ride in.
But only the men go on whale hunts.

Umiaks are
still used today.
What do you think
the rope is for?

An Eskimo hunter on an ice pack

PUBLOK — THERE SHE BLOWS!

One day Akpik climbs up on a tall ice pack.
He is watching for the first whale. Eskimos from
other igloos are getting the things they need to go whaling.
They are getting dogs, sleds, knives, and harpoons.

The hunters are all ready to go just as soon as Akpik sees the whale. They may have to go far out on the ocean. But they do not mind. They want to get as many whales as they can.

Whales mean many good things to the Eskimos:

feasts for Eskimos and dogs,

meat for the winter,

bones for tools,

whale ribs for igloos,

and oil for heat and light.

Eskimos use every bit of the whale, down to the last bit of skin.

To hunt the whale, the hunters use a harpoon. A harpoon is a wooden stick. It has a tip made from a walrus tusk. It has a line made from sealskin. Floats made of sealskin are fastened to the line. We will read about these floats again.

Harpoon and floats

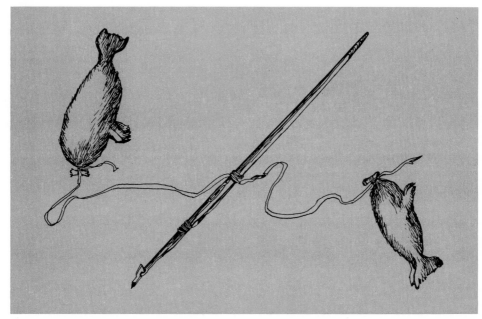

Eskimo hunters of today bringing home a whale. Why don't we have
a photo of whale hunting long ago?

Akpik has been watching from the ice pack
for a long time.   Suddenly he shouts "Publok!"
This means that he sees a whale.   The whale
raises the top of its head out of the water and spouts.

★   Find out why a whale spouts.

When Akpik shouts "Publok," the hunters come running.
The dogs take them to the lead where Akpik saw the whale.
A lead (LEED) is a stream of water that runs where the ice
has pulled apart.   The hunters put the umiak into the water.
They paddle hard.   Akpik is the only one who
does not paddle.   He stands up in the boat.
He must be ready to harpoon the whale when the boat
gets close enough.

Akpik throws the harpoon with all his might.
The ivory tip goes into the whale and stays there.
It hurts the whale.   Down he goes under the water.
With all his might he tugs and pulls.   He twists down
deep in the water.   But he must come up for air.
The sealskin floats stay on top of the water.
They show the hunters where the whale is.
The hunters paddle to the floats as fast as they can.
Soon the whale will come up. And Akpik will be ready
to throw another harpoon.

There is more chasing and harpooning, chasing
and harpooning.   At last the whale is tired out.
Then the hunters kill it.   They pull its body onto the ice.
There they cut it up into big pieces.   Each piece
may weigh as much as 300 pounds.

Muktuk. The black part is skin. The pink part is blubber.

Now the hunters bring home the pieces of whale.
The meat and other parts of the whale are divided up.
Each family gets a share. Everyone is happy.
Once again there is good fresh meat to eat.

The Eskimos store some of the meat in the "freezer."
They save it for the dark months ahead. Then food
will be scarce.

They save every bit of skin. They cut the skin
into pieces. Each piece has some blubber on it.
These pieces are called muktuk. Sometimes
the Eskimos cook the muktuk. Sometimes they
eat it raw.

THE BREAK-UP MONTHS

Now the break-up months begin.   The sun rises
a little higher in the sky.   Snow and ice begin to melt
on the tundra.   Ice on the lakes and rivers begins
to break up.   Now the Eskimos have different work to do.

Ice breaking up in the Arctic Ocean

Break-Up

One morning in the month of May,
  Some birds come flying by.
And later there are many more —
  It makes you wonder why.

Ducks, and ducks, and still more ducks
  Come flying north once more —
Geese and plovers, gulls and terns —
  Across the skies they soar.

Ice on the Arctic Ocean squeaks,
  It makes a lot of noise.
Chunks and hunks of ice break off,
  And float around like toys.

The water comes alive again,
  And whales go bobbing through.
The seals play on the packs of ice —
  And there's a walrus, too!

BIRDS AND BOLAS

Hurry, hurry, hurry! The birds seem to know
that these are the months for building nests, laying eggs,
and hatching baby birds. And there isn't much time.

During the break-up months, hundreds and
hundreds of big birds come. This is when the Eskimos
hunt ducks for food. They know where the ducks fly low
across the tundra. They use bolas to catch them.

Birds nesting on the tundra

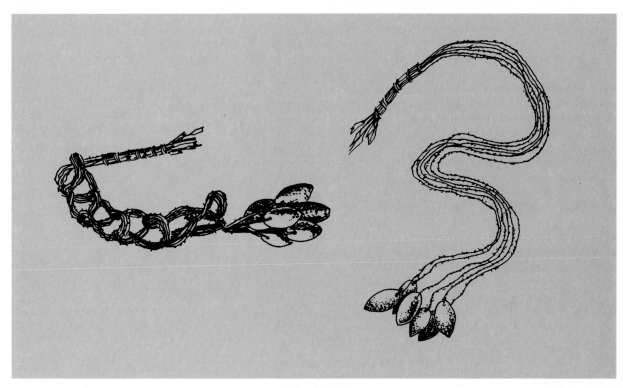

Bolas

A bola is made from lines of sealskin or sinew.
A little ivory ball is tied to the end of each line.
All the lines are tied together at one end
with some feathers. The hunter holds the feathers
in his right hand. When ducks fly by, the hunter
whirls the bola around and around over his head.
Whirr — whirr — whirr! Then he lets go.

The bola flies up and hits one of the ducks. Plop!
Down falls the duck! It is all tangled up in the lines
of the bola. Very quickly the hunter untangles the lines.
He throws the bola again. He has no time to lose.
He must get as many ducks as he can.
He will store them in the "freezer" for the dark months.

Riding in a kayak

THE KAYAK — A LITTLE BOAT

    Eskimos use a big boat called the umiak
on whale hunts. The Eskimos also have a little boat.
It is called a kayak (KI ak).

Only one person can get into a kayak. The kayak is covered with sealskins. The skins are put on so well that not a drop of water can get in.

Kayaks are used during break-up. They are also used when the ice is gone from the rivers and the coast. Akpik uses a kayak when he wants to hunt ducks or seals. He uses a kayak to go fishing. Akpik wears a parka made of sealskin. After he gets into the kayak, he ties his parka around the hole in the boat. How snug he is then! He and his boat are like one.

A kayak is not easy to handle. Often it turns upside down. But a skilled hunter can use his paddle to turn it right-side-up again. Every man and boy must learn to handle a kayak.

Eskimos covering a kayak

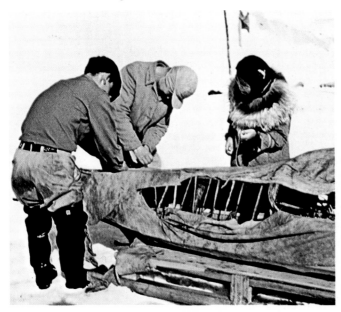

Kayak ready to be used

TIME TO MOVE

Soon the ice will melt on the tundra.
Akpik and his family must move inland from the coast.
Soon they will not be able to get enough food on the coast.
Akpik likes to move when the ice still covers the ground.
Then the dogs and sleds can help.

Akpik's family travels from 50 to 100 miles inland.
They set up their tent beside a river.   Their tent
is made of animal skins.   The skins are put around four
or five poles.   Akpik puts spears, paddles, and oars
against the skins.   This will help to hold them down.

Most of the ice has melted on this part of the tundra.

There is no hole in the top of the tent. The cooking is done outdoors. The family does not need a lamp for heating or lighting. Not much is needed inside the tent. The people spend most of their time outside gathering food.

This is a seal poke. How is it made? How is it used?
Read the next page to find out.

HUNTING SEALS

The Eskimos hunt seals all year long.
But break-up time is the best time for hunting seals.
Then the hunter can get many seals all at once.
This is the seals' favorite time for coming out
on top of the ice to lie in the sun.
The hunter sneaks up when the seals are sleeping.
If he is lucky, he will harpoon a seal. But sometimes
the seal sees the hunter. Then it dives into the ocean.
The hunter is always trying to see which one is quicker —
he or the seal.

Eskimos eat much seal meat. They use sealskins for making boats and boots. Water cannot get through the skins. They use oil from seal blubber for heating igloos.

Sometimes Eskimos skin the seal in one piece. They clean the inside of the skin. Then they tie it shut. This seal "bag" is called a seal poke. The Eskimos use seal pokes to store oil, muktuk, and all kinds of things. Sometimes the seal poke is filled with air and used for a float.

▶ How are floats helpful in hunting whales?

THE GROWING MONTHS

After the break-up months, the growing months begin. The sun rises still higher in the sky. Ice and snow melt. For two short months the weather is warm enough for plants to grow on the tundra.

The village does not look the same as it did long ago. But, of course,
the ice and snow still melt every year during the growing months.

When the Sun Never Sets

The children like to play outdoors,
   They like the golden sun.
They run and jump and laugh and shout,
   And have a lot of fun.

How odd to see the sun so long!
   It does not set at night.
The people do not sleep as much
   Because it is so light.

With so much sunshine day and night
   The plants grow fast, it's true.
However, they are eaten up
   By herds of caribou.

The lemmings eat the grasses, too,
   They nibble here and there.
These brown and furry animals —
   You see them everywhere.

★   Find out more about lemmings.

Lemmings

Arctic flowers

PUDDLES, FLOWERS, BUGS, AND BIRDS

July and August are the growing months.
Moss and grasses grow all over the tundra. Wild flowers
of many different colors grow, too. Tiny willow trees
creep along on top of the ground.

Now there is no ice or snow. But water is everywhere.
Remember, this is the land of permafrost. When the ice
and snow melt, there is no place for the water to go.
There are puddles everywhere. People can never go out
without their boots.

No one likes to travel on the wet tundra.
No one except the mosquitoes. Mosquitoes and
many other kinds of insects are all over the tundra.
They bite animals and people. They are so pesky!
People are glad when freeze-up comes again.

Hundreds of birds come to live on the tundra
during the growing months. It is a good place for them
to raise their families. There is light all the time —
day and night. They can gather more food for the baby birds.

The Eskimos are busy, too. They are gathering food
for their "freezer."

These caribou leg skins are made into mukluks like those of long ago.

What do you think these caribou hides will be used for?

MEN'S WORK

During the growing months, the men go north
to hunt caribou. Caribou travel together. They come north
to the coast to eat the moss and grass. They may stay
only a week. But the men are ready. They kill
as many caribou as they can. They save the
meat and hides. The women will make the hides
into warm clothing.

Every bit of the caribou is used. The bones
are used to make needles, tools, weapons, and knives.
Caribou sinews are used for thread. The antlers
are used for spoons, fishhooks, and spears.

Many walrus come north in the summer. They rest
on the big chunks of ice that float on the ocean. The men
hunt together. They kill as many walrus as they can.
Eskimos do not like walrus meat. But they do store it.
If there is not much other food, they might be glad
to eat the walrus meat. The dogs are not so fussy.
They think walrus meat is just fine to eat — any time!

Fish hanging up to dry

THE WORK OF WOMEN AND CHILDREN

While the men hunt, the women are busy fishing.
They fish by stringing nets across the rivers. This way
they catch many fish. They hang up some to dry.
They put others into the "freezer."

The children set traps to catch little animals.
They help the women hunt ducks and other large birds.
They also find duck eggs and store them.

Sometimes the women and children walk inland
for miles. They look for berries. They eat some
of the berries. The others are stored in oil.

The Eskimos are fond of a food called *akutuk*. It is made of caribou fat and other things. It is a great treat.

★ Why do people who live in very cold climates need more fat in their food than people in warm climates?

People in Barrow today can buy some foods they like at this eating place.

THE FREEZE-UP MONTHS

How quickly the growing months go by!
Soon the tundra begins to freeze up again.
Before the freeze-up months are over, the weather
will be very, very cold.

Getting ready for the freeze-up months

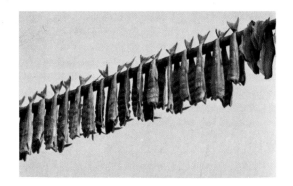

Freeze-Up

The busy, busy months are here —
   There's lots of work to do;
The men and women have to work,
   And all the children, too.

They gather driftwood every day,
   They store all kinds of meat;
For wintertime is long and cold,
   And everyone must eat.

The days are getting shorter now,
   The birds will fly away;
Some animals will wander south,
   Some animals will stay.

The people like the freeze-up months,
   Although the cold winds blow,
Because those pesky insects freeze
   When it begins to snow.

Cutting up a whale

Catching fish

BACK TO THE IGLOO

Now the freeze-up months are here.
It is moving time again. Akpik and his family
move back to the coast. They live in a sod igloo.
It may not be the same igloo they lived in before.

The water and earth on the tundra are beginning
to freeze. So there are many things to be done.
First the igloo must be fixed up. It must be made warm
for the cold winter. It might need more sod
or a new roof.

The Eskimo hunters go out to hunt whales again.
They will cut up the whales and store the meat.
Then they will have food during the winter.

Nets are put out to catch more fish. These fish
are put in the "freezer." If the Eskimos are busy,
they are happy. They are happy because they
are storing food. They will have something to eat
during the hard months ahead.

THE DARK MONTHS

Each day the sun gets lower and lower in the sky. The days get colder and colder. Then one day the sun does not rise at all. There is darkness for two months — day and night. These are the dark months.

Dark Days, Cold Days

The nights are dark, the nights are cold,
    And lonely as can be.
The snow is blowing through the air,
    There's little left to see.

The days are also dark and cold,
    The sun is out of sight.
But even so, as you look out,
    You see an eerie light.

The lakes and streams are solid ice,
    The ocean freezes, too.
The people work and play inside —
    There's nothing else to do.

SEWING, CARVING, AND VISITING

Akpik and his family are back inside their igloo now. They like the dark months if they have enough food. Now they can rest. They can do many things they could not do during the lighter and warmer months.

The women must make new clothes for everyone in the family. The children have time to play. But the girls must watch their mothers. This is how they learn to cook and sew. The boys work right along with their fathers. They learn many things they need to know about hunting.

WOMEN'S TOOLS

comb

skin scraper

knife

Sewing sealskins

Drilling ivory

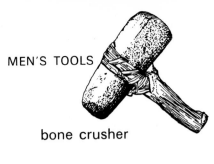

MEN'S TOOLS

bone crusher

goggles

knives

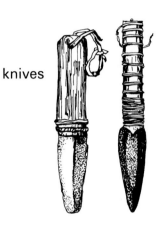

The men spend the dark months at home.
This is when they make new tools and fix up old ones.
They use wood, stone, and ivory. They use bone,
animal skin, and any other things they have found.

The dark months are the months for visiting.
Families like to get together. They just visit
and visit and visit.

Families often get together in the community house.
Here everyone can rest or sing. They can play games
and tell folk tales. A person who tells a tale
acts out the story. The Eskimos of long ago
had no written language. But they told stories
over and over. Everyone learned the stories by heart.

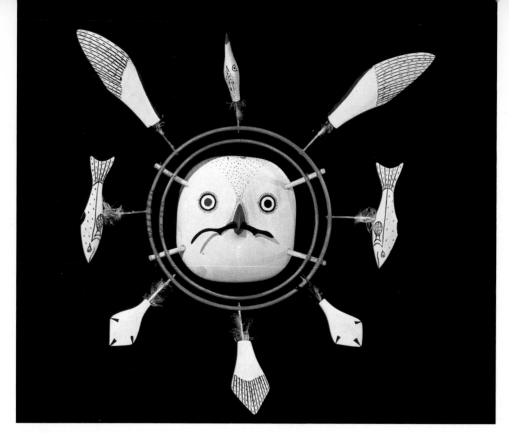

A mask worn by a shaman

THE OLD RELIGION OF THE ESKIMOS

The stories were part of the old religion of the Eskimos.
One folk tale told how the Earth was made by Raven.
Raven was a man. He had a raven's beak
instead of a mouth. Before Raven made the Earth,
there was only water. He made the ground rise
out of the water. Then people could live on it.

The old religion taught that each person has a spirit.
It taught that each animal has a spirit, too.
When an Eskimo man killed an animal, he thought of its
spirit. Then the animal did not mind being killed.
If he did not treat the animal right, its spirit
would tell all the other animals. Then the other animals
would go far away. And the Eskimos would be hungry.

The Eskimos believed that songs were magic. They had songs for everything. Many songs were for hunting. Many were for the weather.

The Eskimos believed in charms, too. Anyone might have a charm. If people wore charms, they would have good luck. Charms could be oogruk claws or polar bear teeth. Even the head of a small animal could be used as a charm.

The Eskimos believed in shamans (SHAH munz). Shamans were Eskimo men or women who seemed to have special power over things or people. Eskimos believed that shamans could do all kinds of things. They could heal sick people. They could find people who are lost. They could tell what is going to happen in the future. They could make special charms for people.

Graveyard

RULES WITHOUT GOVERNMENT

Akpik is the head of his family. He never scolds.
He talks things over with his family. Together they
decide what is right. The children are not punished.
But usually they do not need to be.

Eskimos live together in small groups.
There is no government like ours. There is no chief
or president or king to give orders. But there is a way
of making people do right. Eskimos care very much
what other people think of them. People who
do wrong can be punished. They
may tell the community what they have done.
Then they are ashamed. They try not
to do wrong again.

Eskimos think the older people are wise.
They respect what the older people say.
When something is wrong, it is talked over
with the older people. It is settled the way
the older people think is best.

★ What other people settle their problems
   in this way?

The Eskimos try to follow this rule:
   Do not do anything to your neighbor
   that you would not like him to do to you.

▶ Have you heard a rule like this before?

120

THE ESKIMO CULTURE

In this chapter, you learned about the old culture of the Eskimos.   A **culture** is a way of life.

The culture of any community lets the people make a living.   It gives them a religion.   It helps them to have fun.   It gives them rules for living together.   Children learn the culture as they grow. Later, they pass the culture on to *their* children.

- Review the Eskimo culture, using these questions:
  What do Eskimos look like?
  What kind of family life did they have?
  How did they dress?
  What kinds of houses did they have?
  What food did they eat?
  What was their religion?
  What work did men, women, and children do?
  How did children learn?
  How did the Eskimos have fun?
  What rules and government did they have?
  Did their way of life change much?
  What transportation did they have?

Does this picture show the tundra today or long ago? How can you tell?

CHAPTER **7**
How the Eskimos Live Today

BARROW TODAY

Do you remember Dixie? She is the Eskimo dog who went to live in Ohio.

▶ Where did Dixie live before she went to Ohio?

We have learned something about Dixie's old home. We have learned how Eskimos used to live there. We have learned how they used animals for clothing, food, and shelter. We know how hard it was for them to find food. They had little time for anything else.

Barrow twenty years ago
Barrow today

Now let us visit Dixie's old home again.
We will see Barrow as it is today. We will see
how the lives of Eskimos there are changing.

Barrow is the largest Eskimo community
in the world.

Look closely at the pictures.

● Find some changes that have taken place.

The buildings in Barrow are on the tundra.
They are along the coast of the Arctic Ocean.
Eskimos live in them all year round.
They no longer move away to look for food
as they did years ago.

Some Eskimos work in the village of Barrow.
Most of the children go to school in the village.

Alaskan children in school. Some are Eskimos.
What language do they all learn?

The only igloo in Barrow. Do you see the meat hanging on the rack?

SHELTER

In Barrow the Eskimos live in houses made of wood.
Inside each house is an oil stove for cooking
and heating. A gas line has been put into Barrow.
Now the people can use gas stoves.

Once there were many igloos in Barrow.
Now there is only one left. An Eskimo lives in it.

Eskimos used to move from their igloos into tents.
Even today, Eskimos like to live in tents when it is warm.
They put up tents beside their houses. But today
the tents are made of canvas cloth instead of skins.

Eskimo summer tents. How are these tents different from tents used long ago?

An Eskimo house in Barrow

There is a hospital in Barrow. Eskimos go
to the hospital to get shots. They go there
when they need special care.

There are also three churches in Barrow.
Many Eskimos go to church.

● Is the religion of the Eskimos changing?

FOOD

Many years ago, Eskimo men spent most
of their time hunting. They had to hunt animals
for food. Today many Eskimo men have jobs.
So they cannot spend most of their time hunting.

Whale, seal, and caribou are still the main foods
of the Eskimos. The men hunt these animals when they
are not working at their jobs. The meat is cut up.
It is still stored in the underground "freezers,"
just as it was years ago. Oil and blubber
are still stored in sealskin pokes.

Eskimo men and women buy many things at
the stores in Barrow. The women buy flour, sugar,
tea, and coffee. They buy canned foods.

More changes will be made as other foods
are brought to the stores. Every day a plane
flies into Barrow. It carries fruit, eggs, vegetables,
and fresh meat.

Hospital in Barrow   The first church built in Barrow

What are some things Eskimos can buy in this store?

An Eskimo girl wearing clothes
bought in a store

CLOTHING

Many Eskimo women still sew much
of the clothing for their families.
But today they use sewing machines.
When the women sew by hand, they do not use
needles made of bone. They use steel needles.
They buy these needles at the store.

An Eskimo still wears one suit
with the fur inside. But now the second one
is a brightly colored one made of cotton cloth.

In warmer months the tundra is
just as wet as ever. Eskimos today use
rubber boots for walking in the slush
and mud.

THE WORK OF WOMEN

Earlier, you learned about the work
of women long ago. They fished, hunted,
gathered food, cooked, and made clothes.
Today, Eskimo women do many new jobs.
Women in other parts of Alaska are doing
new things.

● Can you name some?

Two happy grandmothers in their cotton dresses

Making a trip to the post office

Eskimos fixing a motor

NEW WISHES FOR NEW THINGS

All Eskimo families in Barrow have
mail-order catalogs. Catalogs show things
that are sold in stores in the cities.
Families may have 2 or 3 catalogs. They call
these catalogs their wish books. Eskimos
spend hours looking through their wish books.
They wish for many things they see. But it takes
money to order these things from the store.

When they have money, Eskimos order many things.
They send for cloth, knives, guns, and motors.
They send for tents, toys, and clothing.

Many people in Barrow have used their money
to buy snowmobiles. Very few ever travel
by dogsled today. Snowmobiles are a faster
way to travel.

Small planes on the airstrip in Barrow

An even faster way to travel is by airplane.
Many Alaskans own small planes. Barrow now
has an airstrip for them.

Eskimos still use umiaks for hunting whales.
Now they put motors on the boats. They also use
motorboats.

The Eskimos can write their language in letters
like these. Children write to their friends. They
use English or the Eskimo language, *Inupiag*.

Many Eskimos have bought tape recorders.
Instead of writing letters, they record their voices.
Then they can send the tapes in the mail.

A family takes a ride in a boat with a motor.

ART

People can find time for art even when they have to spend most of their time finding food. Today, the Eskimos in Barrow have more time for art. Some of them make drawings. The women decorate their parkas with beautiful designs. They make sure that no two designs are alike. Eskimos also make pretty baskets out of baleen.

▶ From what animal does baleen come?

Eskimo sculpture made of ivory

A parka design

A basket made from baleen. The handle is a walrus
carved from ivory.

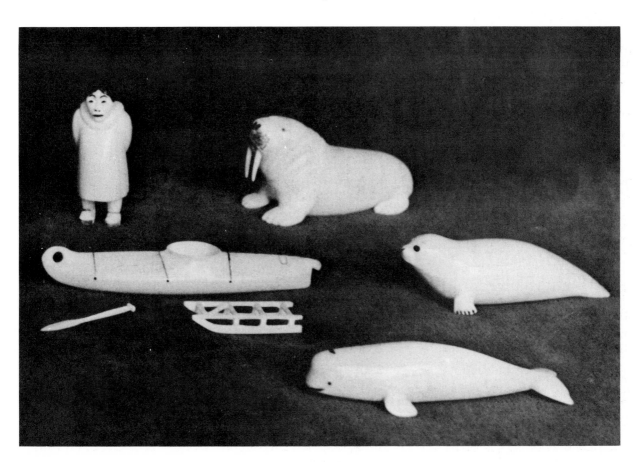

Alaskan drummers

MUSIC

Eskimos love music. Their music has not changed
very much. They still sing songs about hunting
and animals. Sometimes they just make musical sounds.

Their favorite musical instrument is a drum.
The drum is made of a hoop of willow. Its handle
is made of walrus tusks, caribou antler, or wood.
Caribou skin is stretched tightly over the hoop.

The Eskimo uses a short wooden drumstick
to play the drum. It is wrapped with sealskin.
The player hits a willow hoop:

> 1, 2, 3, 4 — 1, 2, 3, 4.

Some of the young people have record players.
Many of them like to play "rock and roll" records.
They like American folk songs, too.

A dogsled race

FUN FOR EVERYONE

The Eskimos still enjoy singing and dancing.
They still enjoy storytelling. When work is done,
they love to visit. They go to someone's house.
They sit and talk and drink tea.

Eskimos like to have feasts. They always have
a feast after a whale is caught. First they eat.
Then they sing, dance, and play games.

One game is called blanket toss,
or nalukatak (NAH luk ah TAHK). The Eskimos hold up
a blanket of walrus hide. They toss people up
into the air. Higher and higher and higher
they go! They try to land on their feet. If they
do not land on their feet, they fall down
in the blanket. Then the Eskimos shout and laugh.
They have lots of fun.

The Eskimos also like
to play games that help them
become strong. They walk
on their hands. They do stunts
on ropes. They wrestle,
jump, and play kickball.

Eskimos think races
are a lot of fun! They like
to run foot races.
They have dogsled races
and boat races, too.

Blanket toss

Children playing

The Capitol in Washington, D.C. Lawmakers work here for the whole country.

CHANGES IN GOVERNMENT

Alaska is one of the 50 United States.
That means it has the same president and
the same capital that all Americans have.
The people in Barrow are American citizens,
just like people in your community. They may vote and
help choose the president and the lawmakers.
The Eskimos are proud to be citizens of the United States.

Do you remember learning about the government in your
own community? Barrow has a government
for its community, too. It has a mayor and a council.
They make the rules and laws.

For a long time the Eskimos lived
with very different rules. They had no government.
People understood how they were to live.
They were used to living that way. Now they
are proud to be citizens. They obey the laws.

- Why should people obey the laws? What happens
  when people do not obey rules and laws?

This woman is a United States judge in Barrow.

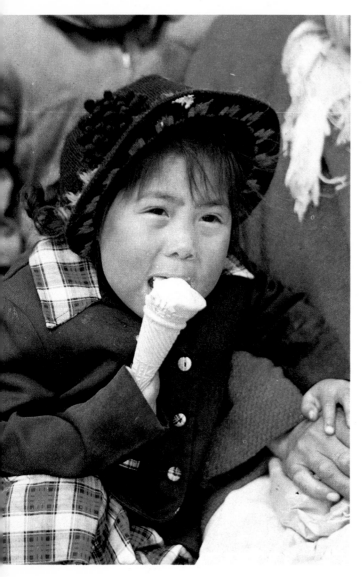

Look at the pictures. Can you tell
some of the changes that have come
to the Eskimos?

WHY CHANGES CAME

The culture of the Eskimos changed little
for thousands of years. Then it began to change fast.
Why did so much change come to the Eskimos?

Many years ago, people did not know very much
about Alaska. Many people in the United States
wanted whale oil and baleen. To get whales,
people went to Barrow.

Later, the United States bought Alaska from Russia.
Gold was found in Alaska. Many people moved there.
Still later, many soldiers came to Alaska.

When all these people came to Alaska, they met
the Eskimos. Eskimos learned how people in other parts
of the world lived. They wanted many of the things
that these people had. Eskimos needed money to get
these things. They had to make some changes
in their ways of living.

- Why did Eskimos need money?

- What were some of the changes
  in their ways of living?

IS CHANGE GOOD OR BAD FOR THE ESKIMOS?

Has change helped or hurt the Eskimos?

The people live much longer. They do not die from hunger. They can buy food and other things at the stores. Most of them have houses that are heated. They have a hospital and schools. Many are learning new skills.

Some of the changes are not so helpful. Some Eskimos get sick from diseases brought by people who have just come to Alaska.

The Eskimos used to have good teeth. But now they eat candy and other sweets. Their teeth decay.

Some of the Eskimos have forgotten the skills of their mothers and fathers. Some have not learned new skills. Without new skills, Eskimos cannot do new kinds of work. So some cannot find jobs.

● Do you think change for the Eskimos was more good than bad? Why?

CULTURE SHOCK

When people meet a new culture they sometimes have **culture shock.** This means that they feel upset by all the new ideas and new things. Many Eskimos had culture shock when they first met people whose culture came from Europe.

- Can you see why this is called culture shock? What is a shock?

- Think about Akpik's family. Should the Eskimos give up all their old culture?

- Have you ever had something like culture shock? Moving to a new community can be a tiny culture shock. So can going to a new school. Might these shocks be hard to handle? Why or why not?

- You know about Eskimo children. What other children in the United States sometimes have a big culture shock? What about Indian children? Children who speak Spanish? Children who move from a farm to a big city? What can others do for children with culture shock? How can they be helped?

- Will the changing role of women cause culture shock?

THE PROBLEM OF ALASKA'S ENVIRONMENT

There is a big problem in Alaska today.
It is this: How can we save the natural environment?

▶ How did Eskimos use wild animals?

● What would have happened if the Eskimos
had killed all the seals or whales?

Today wild animals are in danger. They are
being killed too fast. Fast ships with harpoon guns
kill whales by the thousand. Soon there may be
no whales left.

The Eskimos *needed* skins and furs. They
needed them to keep warm in the bitter cold. Today,
many people wear furs just for show. Seals and
other fur animals may all be killed.

A whaling ship today

There is a new problem, too. Companies are drilling oil wells in northern Alaska.

● How do oil wells change the environment?

The oil must be carried to other parts of the United States and to Europe. This will be done by big tankers. But tankers cannot sail from the north coast of Alaska. The water near the coast is not deep enough. The Arctic Ocean is frozen nearly all the year round.

Tankers *can* sail from the south coast of Alaska. But the south coast is more than 700 miles away from the oil wells.

People decided to build a pipeline from north Alaska to the south.

★ What is a pipeline? How is oil pumped through a pipeline?

This is part of the Alaska Pipeline.

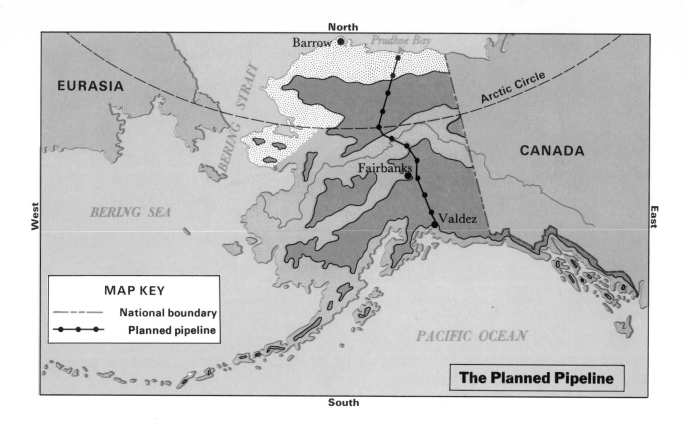

The Planned Pipeline

The pipeline will be 789 miles long and
4 feet wide. It will carry 2 million barrels
of oil a day.

- Many people think the pipeline will harm
  the environment badly. What kinds of harm
  might it do?

Think of:

      Leaks in the pipeline
      Harm to plants and animals and fish
      Melting the permafrost
      Indian and Eskimo communities

The people who plan the pipeline think they can save the environment.

They plan *cut-offs* that will turn off the oil if there is a leak.

They will put back plants and soil.

They will plan crossing places for animals.

They will build the pipeline so as not to melt the permafrost.

They will train Indians and Eskimos to work on the pipeline.

● Still, many people think the pipeline is a mistake.   What do you think?

There will be a highway near the pipeline. How would a highway affect living things in Alaska's natural environment?

Don't Have Culture Shock!

If you travel around the world,
    To see where other people dwell,
You may have quite a culture shock
    Unless you've studied well!

Can you eat a slice of blubber raw?
    Can you chew a witchetty grub?
Or throw a spear? Or chase a deer?
    Or catch a koala cub?

Would you defrost the permafrost?
    Would you laugh at a shaman's mask?
Is a churinga good to eat?
    What questions would you ask?

Communities have ways of life,
    Beliefs, and many a rule.
And if you don't want culture shock,
    You'll study well at school!

Part Two

REVIEW

CHAPTER **1**

The Earth and the Sun

EARTH

You have learned many things about the Earth. Tell what you remember.

▶ What is the Earth?

▶ What shape is the Earth?

▶ What is a model of the Earth called?

▶ Name the continents on the Earth.

▶ Name the four oceans.

▶ What living things are on the Earth?

THE EQUATOR AND THE POLES

Use your globe for these questions:

▶ Find the Equator. What is the Equator?

▶ Find the North Pole. What is the North Pole?

▶ Find the South Pole. What is the South Pole?

Use the pictures to answer these questions:

▶ Who lives nearest the Equator?

▶ Who lives nearest the North Pole?

▶ Who lives nearest the South Pole?

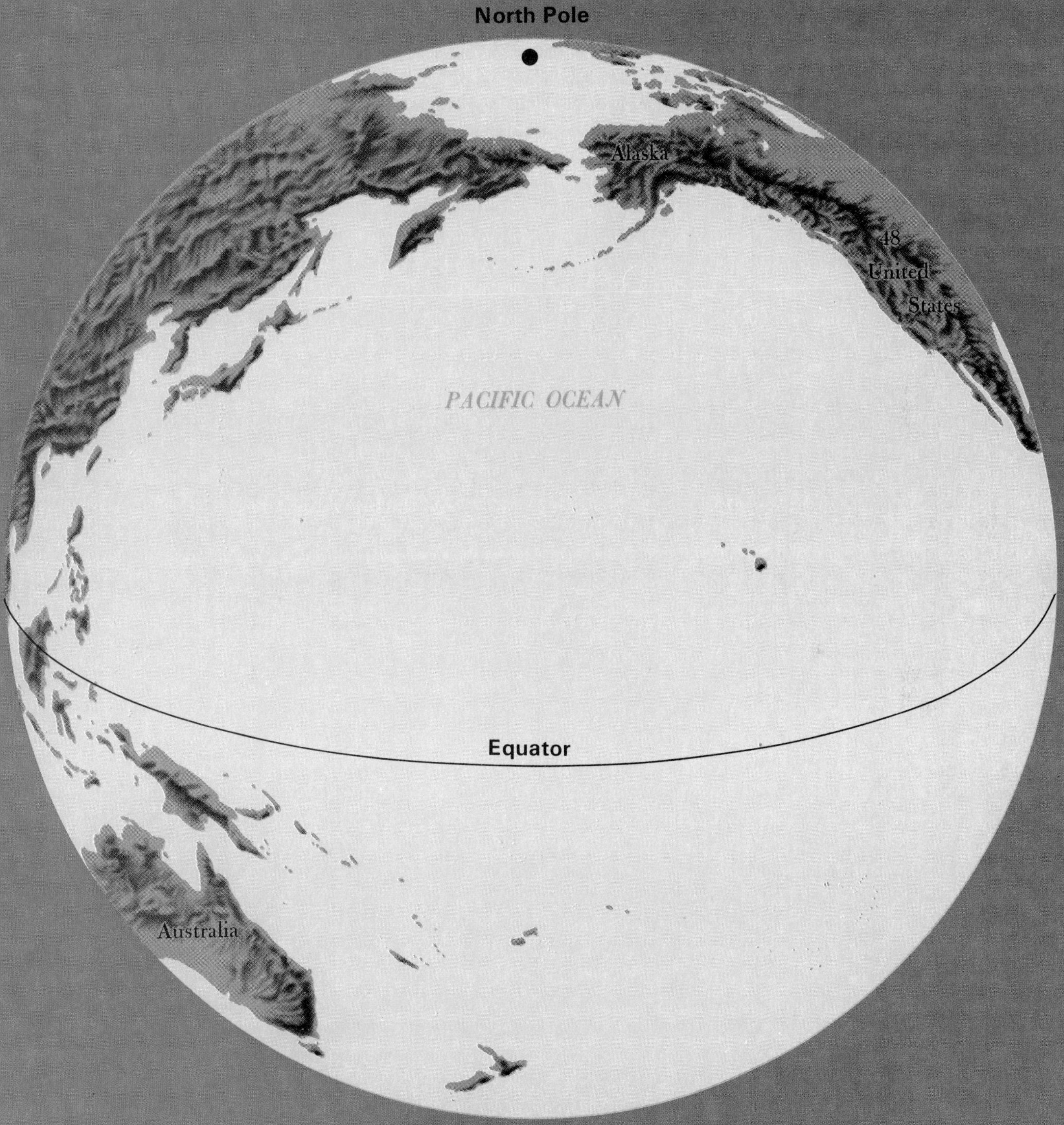

North Pole

Alaska

48
United
States

PACIFIC OCEAN

Equator

Australia

Where is the South Pole?

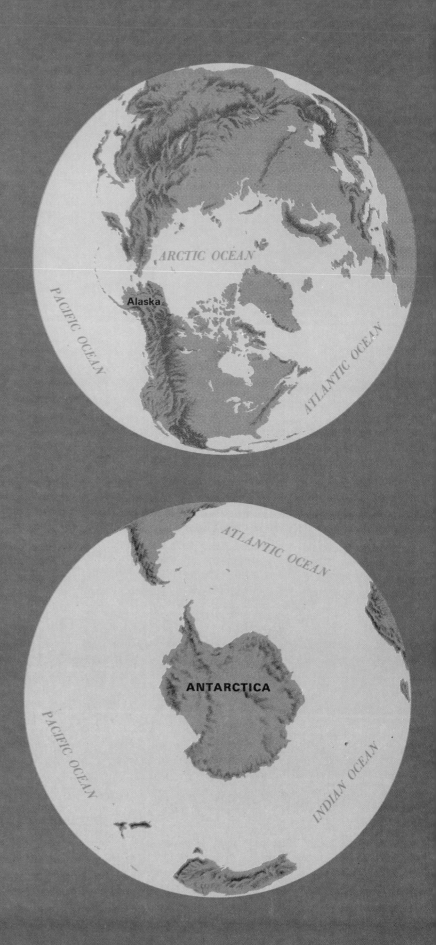

Is this around
the North Pole or
the South Pole?

Is this around
the North Pole or
the South Pole?

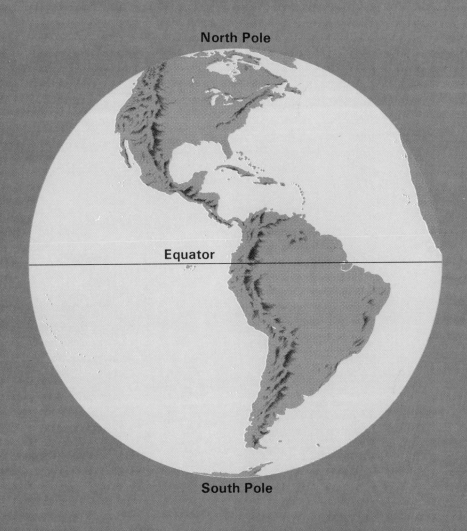

North Pole

Equator

South Pole

HEMISPHERES

▶ What is a hemisphere?

▶ What hemisphere is north of the Equator?

▶ Name a continent in this hemisphere.

▶ What hemisphere is south of the Equator?

▶ Name a continent in this hemisphere.

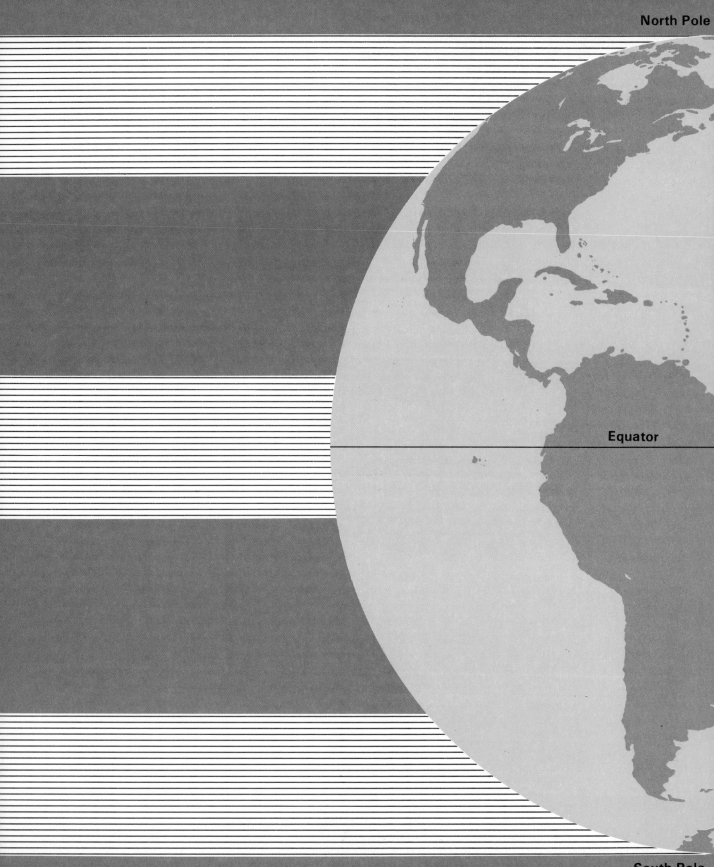

North Pole

Equator

South Pole

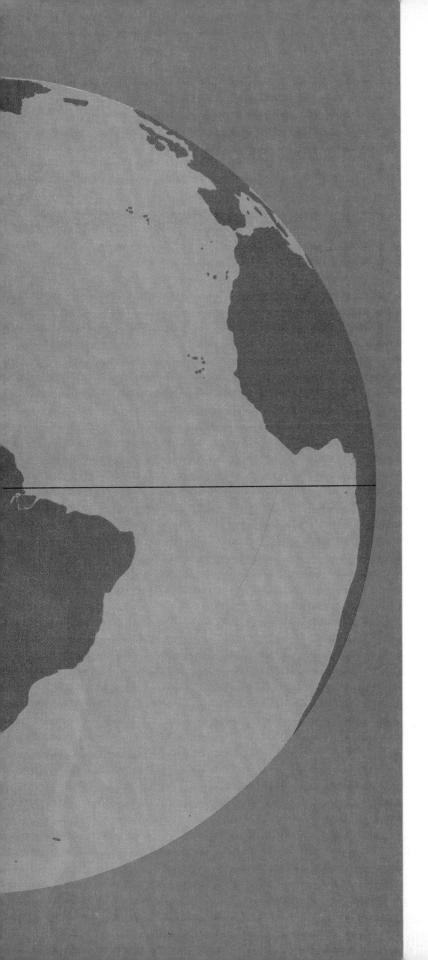

EARTH AND SUN

▶ What do the sun's rays
bring to the Earth?

▶ Where is the sun
high in the sky all year —
at the Equator
or at the Poles?

▶ Where is the sun
low in the sky all year —
at the Equator
or at the Poles?

▶ Which lands
on the Earth
are warmer —
lands near the Equator
or lands near the Poles?
Why?

▶ What about lands
between the Equator
and the Poles?

CLIMATE

▶ Which picture shows a place that gets the most rain?

▶ Which pictures show places that get very little rain?

► Which pictures show places
that are cold all year?

► Which picture shows a place
that is warm all year?

► In which place does the weather
change very much during the year?

| Mountains | River | Tundra |

PHYSICAL FEATURES

Physical features can be shown on maps and globes.

▶ What physical features can you find on this map?

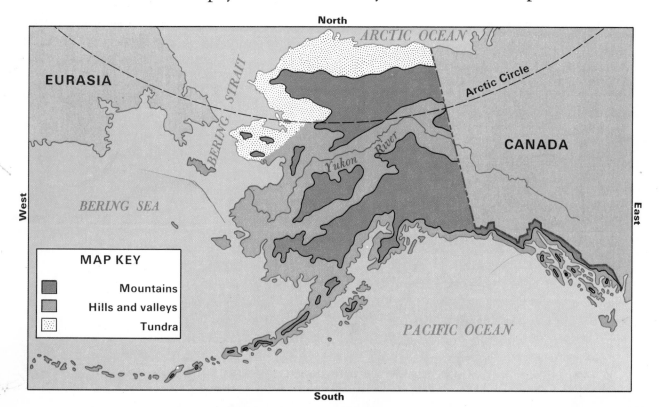

City of Sydney   Airport   Railroad

CULTURAL FEATURES

Cultural features can be shown on maps and globes.

▶ What cultural features can you find on this map?

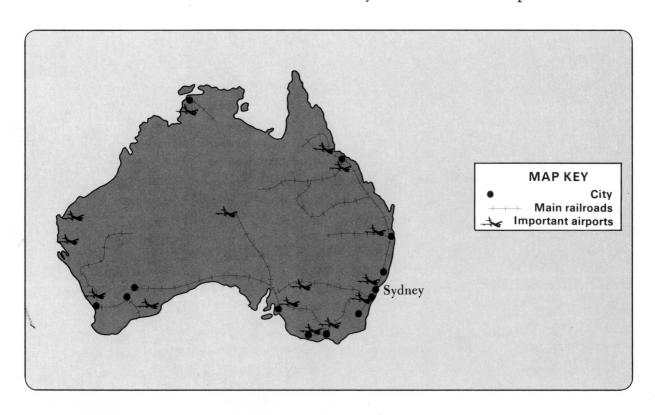

MAP KEY
●   City
+++++   Main railroads
✈   Important airports

Sydney

CHAPTER 2
Communities and Cultures

PEOPLE ON THE EARTH

People live in many lands. Most of them live on the landmasses. Many live on islands.

They live in communities. Each community has its place. It may be somewhere on a landmass or continent. It may be somewhere on an island.

▶ Name some communities on a continent.

▶ Name a community on an island.

Each place on Earth has its own natural environment. Natural environments can be very different.

▶ Can you remember the *four parts* of the natural environment?

● Give examples of different natural environments.

THE CULTURE OF A COMMUNITY

Every community has a culture — whole way of living. The culture helps people to live and work together.

- How do children learn about their community?

- How are you learning about your culture?

- Does learning about other cultures help you? How?

- What is culture shock?

- Give examples of cultural features that make big changes in the environment.

- Use the picture chart on pages 167–170 to compare your community and the Eskimo community of Barrow, Alaska.

COMPARING CULTURES

1. What do the people look like? What clothes do they wear? What are their families like?

2. What houses do they have?

3. What food do they eat?

4. What work do they do? How do they
   get goods and services?

5. What is their religion?

 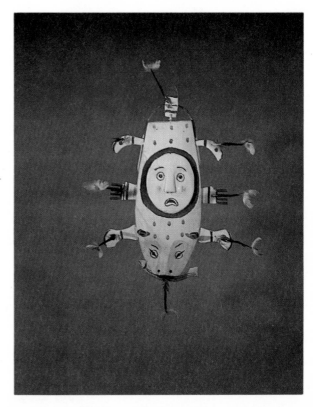

6. What fun do they have? What art and stories?

7. How do children learn?

8. What rules and government do they have?

9. What was the community like long ago?
Is it changing fast?